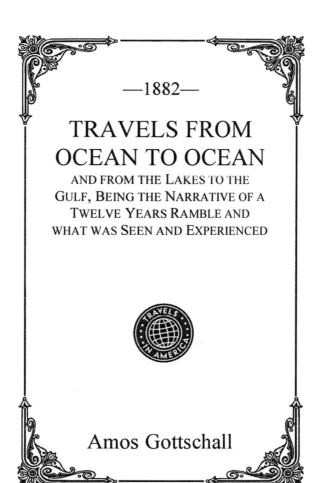

—1882—

TRAVELS FROM OCEAN TO OCEAN

AND FROM THE LAKES TO THE
GULF, BEING THE NARRATIVE OF A
TWELVE YEARS RAMBLE AND
WHAT WAS SEEN AND EXPERIENCED

Amos Gottschall

Volume 187

APPLEWO

Carlisle, M

First Edition

ISBN: 1-4290-0449-5 (Paperback)

For a free copy of our current print catalog, write to:
Applewood Books
PO Box 365
Bedford, MA 01730

For more complete listings,
visit us on the web at:
awb.com

TRAVELS

FROM

OCEAN TO OCEAN,

AND FROM

THE LAKES TO THE GULF;

BEING

THE NARRATIVE OF
A TWELVE YEARS' RAMBLE, AND WHAT
WAS SEEN AND EXPERIENCED:

EMBRACING

Journeys East, West, North, South, Life and Scenes in the Mountains,
upon the Prairies, and along the Lakes and Rivers of the West;
Tours with Buffalo-Hunters; Travels among the Indians; Their
Life and Habits Described; Strolls in the Cotton-Fields,
Orange-Groves, and Forests of the "Sunny South,"
with Notes on Southern Life and Scenery; also
a description of various Cities and Towns in
the United States visited by the Writer.

BY THE AUTHOR OF
"The Chippewa's Last Turn," and *"Sioux Camp"*

THIRD EDITION.

HARRISBURG, PENN.:
AMOS H. GOTTSCHALL, PUBLISHER.
1882.

ELECTROTYPED BY FERGUSON BROTHERS & CO., PHILADELPHIA, PA.

PREFACE.

READER, this is a narrative of my travels and adventures, written in a plain, unvarnished style. It is said that "Truth is stranger than fiction," and, without egotism, (I am devoid of personal vanity) I believe that my worldly experience, for width and ever-changing phases, has been exceeded by that of few men of my years.

Having ran away from home in early boyhood, and being a wanderer for twelve years, my life has been one of singular experiences, and full of "ups and downs."

The work was written under widely-contrasting circumstances. In Indian camps, amid the scenes of savage life; on the puffing steamboat and the rushing cars; on the prairie and the mountain; on the placid lake and the ever-restless ocean; in the printing-office and the jostling hotel; in the lonely forest and amid the city's din; by the roaring cataract and the silent river; in the hut of the hunter and pioneer, and in the parlor of civilization.

While I trust that the book will be entertaining, I am confident that it embodies a wholesome lesson

(iii)

for all runaway-inclined-boys, and all persons of a roving, dissatisfied disposition, as well as being a useful and instructive book in giving a description of people, things and places, as I found them.

It is one thing to sit at home by the cozy fireside and read a traveler's narrative, and, in the imagination, follow him through all of his experiences, but it is quite another thing to fully appreciate them.

I am frequently asked whether I regret the time I spent in roving, and my answer is invariably this: "No; but I would not again go through and endure what fell to my lot for the wealth of kings!"

My journeys have led me into every state in the Union, but one, and into nearly all of the Western Territories, into every city and town of importance in the United States, and into the country of the Pawnee, Shoshonee, Ute, Pahute, Digger, Sioux, Ponca, Arickaree, Chippewa, Winnebago, and other Indians, among whom I have lived and traveled.

Four times have I crossed the North American Continent from the Atlantic to the Pacific, have made five tours through the Southern States, and beside these, I have taken various separate trips to the Sioux Indians of Dakota.

With eyes and pencil ever on the alert, I made a note of whatever I observed which I deemed would make my book entertaining and useful, and I now place my humble efforts before, I hope, a very kind-judging and appreciative public.

CONTENTS.

CHAPTER VI.

CONTENTS.

CHAPTER XVII.

CHAPTER XVIII.

CHAPTER XIX.

CHAPTER XX.

CHAPTER XXI.

NARRATIVE OF TRAVELS.

CHAPTER I.

> An old farm-house with meadows wide,
> And sweet with clover on each side;
> A bright-eyed boy, who looks from out
> The door with woodbine wreathed about,
> And wishes his one thought all day:
> "Oh! if I could but fly away
> From this dull spot the world to see,
> How happy I should be!"
>
> Amid the city's constant din,
> A man who round the world has been,
> Who, 'mid the tumult and the throng,
> Is thinking, thinking all day long:
> "Oh! could I only tread once more
> The field-path to the farm-house door;
> The old, green meadow could I see,
> How happy I should be!"
>
> ANON.

EARLY HISTORY—WHEN A CHILD I DESIRE TO TRAVEL.—HINTS AND SUGGESTIONS FOR DISSATISFIED BOYS—I RUN AWAY FROM HOME WHEN TEN YEARS OLD—REGRETS ON LEAVING MOTHER—HOW I FELT ABOUT GOING HOME—THE ADVICE OF A SEAMAN—PRECIOUS IS THE MEMORY OF CHILDHOOD—THE SELFISHNESS OF HUMAN NATURE—BOOKS AS FRIENDS.

I WAS born in the year 1854, near Lancaster, Pennsylvania. Early in life the desire to leave my home, and see the world and its people outside of my quiet, narrow sphere, was the leading theme of my childish thoughts and plans.

(9)

To be able, sometime in the future, to live with the Indians in their native wilds, and to travel over the vast extent of country between the Atlantic and the Pacific, and the Great Lakes and the Gulf of Mexico, was my aim and object even from the time I could read a book or understand a map.

When the news of the trouble with the Sioux, at New Ulm, Minnesota, in 1862, reached my home, I was only eight years old, but the stories that I had heard about the Indians, and their wild, nomadic life, so impressed my young mind, that I resolved to see and know these people. My fondest hopes have been fully realized, and I now wish in vain for the happy, serene experience of my childhood days.

When a little school-boy, I read the poem which heads this chapter, and I well remember that I, at the time, wondered whether I would, like the subject of the poem, ever see so much of the world that I would become weary of its animation, and long for the peaceable country life which I was so eager to leave—such, indeed, is now my experience.

"Amid the city's constant din," where the shifting circumstances of life have called me to take up my abode, my mind often dwells upon my joyous boyhood days, and the lovely meadows and fields of my early country home, with those poetical, hallowed feelings that raise the soul above its prison-house of clay, and seem to usher it into channels above this bustling world.

A longing to live with the Indians, and to travel and see the country, is a folly from which few boys are exempt; yet no life so abounds with hardships.

Very few travelers, as a rule, become fully tired of roving. Generally speaking, the more a person sees, the more they desire to see, consequently the contented mind and happiness of a man who never cared to roam, is unknown to the restless traveler.

Remember, boys, it is one thing to sit behind the stove at home, and "build air castles" about leaving home to go out into the world, but quite another thing to find the kind of experience you anticipate. Outside of your home and immediate circle of real friends, you will find this to be a very cold, unappreciative, thoughtless, selfish world.

Accept the admonition of one who has "lived and learned." Stay at home! At least never leave it with the sole intention of "seeing the world." The happiest and most contented people are those who are not slaves to a roving disposition and a discontented mind, and are blessed with that earthly paradise of love, peace and comfort—a happy home.

When I recall the many narrow escapes I made from a sudden death, I am convinced that a kind, lenient Providence led me safely through, and He who sees our inner being, knows that henceforth I am determined to discard the fading things of this life, and cheerfully tread that "narrow path" which leads to the "Land of immortality."

Books and papers were always far more desirable
companions to me, than gay and giddy company,
hence, I was generally considered a quiet, old-fashioned boy, a title which I suppose is still appropri-
ate, for an increase of years and worldly experience
has taught me, that while deep and unassuming people are seldom understood or appreciated by those
shallow souls whose entire depth of thought and
mind is ever on their tongue's end, quiet, observing
men and women are generally more successful in
the end.

It is very noticeable, too, that real, genuine sociability, charitable intent and kindness of heart, are
much more generally found among them, than it is
among the other class.   But we are all here together, and should live in peace and harmony, one with
another.   While we do not admire the thoughtless
and giddy, we will endeavor to overlook their weakness with charity.

To some of my readers, the above assertions may
seem like self-laudation or irony, but such is far
from being the case; for it is prompted by an humble heart, and one, that I trust, abounds in love
and sympathy for its fellow beings.   The right-
thinking reader will at once recognize the spirit
in which it was written.

But I must return to the actual thread of my narrative.   Thoughts of running away from home, and
plans for carrying them out, filled my mind at an

early age. My parents, seeing the drift of my inclinations, and knowing to what they would lead,
did all in their power to convince me that I should
banish them; but all their counsel and expostula-
tions were in vain.

Finally, I concluded to run away; and in the
month of July, 1864, when in my tenth year, I left
my kind, loving mother, father, sisters and brothers, to face the storms and rebuffs of this cold, un-
friendly world.

The anguish and suffering this cruel act caused
my mother, cannot well be described. None but a
mother can realize it. I have since often wondered how I could be so ungrateful as to cause that
mother, who had never shown me aught but loving
kindness, so much sorrow and anxiety by my way-
wardness and disobedience. But thus it is in life,
our past errors and short-comings are ever a source
of remorse and regret to us.

One bright, sunny day, while playing with my
little sister, near our home in Marietta, Pennsylvania, the thought occurred to me that the time had
now come for me to start out and see the world. I
was bare-footed at the time, and not wanting to
travel in that condition, I slyly pretended to my
sister that the pebbles on the river bank, where I
had promised to take her, would hurt my feet, and
requested her to run home and get my shoes.

Not knowing my intentions, she started for the

house immediately, and when she returned with the
shoes, I made some excuse to get away from her,
and when out of her sight, I started off as fast as
my limbs could carry me, going I scarcely knew
where—but to see the country, as I supposed.

The first night I stopped at the house of a Mr.
Henry Sheirich, a short distance below Mount-
ville, and nine miles from my home, having been
left at that place by a railroad conductor who was
unwilling to carry a little boy that was traveling
away from home, and could not give a good account of himself.

The wife of Mr. Sheirich was much surprised
to find such a young boy out in the world alone,
and her kind, motherly attention reminded me of
home and my own mother, whom I knew was in
painful suspense, wondering what had become of
her boy.

I managed to keep up spirits pretty well during
the day, but when evening came, and the gentle
voice of my mother calling me from play, did not
greet me as usual, I felt much depressed. When
bedtime arrived, and there was no kind mother to
give me a "good-night kiss," I heartily wished myself in my own little bed at home.

When I awoke, the sun was shining brightly, and
that, with the other cheering influences of a beautiful summer morning in the country, greatly revived
my drooping spirits. The night before, I had al-

most resolved to turn back, but now my good reso-
lution departed entirely.

Bidding my hosts adieu, I walked to Lancaster,
where I took the cars for the Gap, a small village
about fifteen miles distant. I paid my fare with
the little savings of pocket-money which I had laid
by for a traveling fund, though the whole amount
in store was but a few dollars.

I found an uncle at the Gap, and surprised him
more than a little, but I managed to make some excuse for being alone, which I supposed satisfied
him, but he knew considerable more about boys
than I did, and had his own opinion as to the manner in which I had left home.

After remaining a week, I started for home, to all
appearances, but I left the cars at Lancaster, intending to go some other direction the next day.
That night I stopped at Shober's Hotel, and while
waiting to be shown to a room, a son of the proprietor began to question me in a way that put me
ill at ease, and after a few remarks, he said:

"I know your father well, and there is an advertisement here in the *Lancaster Express*, which, I
think, concerns you, as a lost boy of your name
and description is wanted by his parents at Marietta; but go to bed now, and in the morning I will
see that you get home."

I could not well deny that I was the boy referred
to in the advertisement, and I started for my room

feeling rather "crest-fallen." The room which had been assigned me happened to be one that I had once occupied with my father, while visiting the city with him, and it served to remind me of parents and home.

The next morning, I arose very early and left the house, for sorry as I now was that I had left home, I did not want to be taken back as a "runaway-boy." Sometime during the day I visited an aunt, who was living near the city, and after remaining a few days, she succeeded in making me promise to return to my parents and be a good boy.

To run away was easy enough, but to go back again, after leaving in that way, and acknowledge my fault, did not seem near so easy. I arrived at Marietta toward evening, but I did not start for home till dark, and then I walked in the middle of the street, for I did not want any of my playmates to have any fun at my expense just then.

Upon reaching the house, I had not sufficient courage to go in. The door was open, and between the palings of the yard fence, I could see my father reading by the evening lamp, but my mother was not present, and I grew mournfully sad with bitter reflections. Crouched there in the dark, so sad and unhappy, these thoughts came to my mind, "Well, it looks as though they can get along without me, and I guess I am not their boy any more, and so I might as well go way again."

The next morning, however, I walked into the yard where my father was picking pears, and by way of introducing myself, I said: "Well, how do they turn out?"

"Pretty well," he replied, "but where have you been?" he asked.

"Why, I was down to see uncle Henry," I answered, with as much composure as I could.

By this time my mother and sisters, hearing my voice, came out to greet the "prodigal." Mother, of course, first thought of giving me some breakfast, but father (fathers are never so forgiving, kind and thoughtful, as mothers are) thought that the first and most important thing to give me, just then was a lecture.

Everything was now past and forgiven, but I did not appreciate it. The desire to travel and see the world, was as strong as ever, and two weeks after my return, all my promises and resolutions were discarded, and I stole away from home and went to Philadelphia, riding from Lancaster in a freight-car loaded with leaf-tobacco in boxes, and a sultry, uncomfortable ride it was.

For several days I wandered up and down the streets, seeing the sights of the great metropolis, and lingering about the ships at the wharves. All was new, strange and wonderful to me, and I noted the various and amazing phases of city life, with all the gaping astonishment of the country boy on his first visit to the city. The city's splendor, life, din and confusion, however, has now no charm for me, and I love the calm, quiet, peaceful country.

The yearning desire of my boyhood days was to see the world as it existed outside of my quiet home and narrow sphere, but the desire has been entirely satisfied; and after more than an ordinary worldly experience, for one of my years, I have come to realize that one of the greatest degrees of earthly happiness is obtained by the unsophisticated, free and joyous country boy at home. I have learned that we can become thoroughly goaded with our own desires.

A home in the country is the most beautiful and enchanting of all earthly homes. Here we are far more with Nature, and can have sweet communion with the firmament, the forests, the streams, the birds, the flowers! A true home, where love, confidence and kind thoughtfulness for the comfort of others exist, must surely, to some extent at least, resemble Heaven itself, where all is love, peace and harmony.

One day, while in Philadelphia, I found an uncle who was living on Arch Street, and I presented myself to him looking rather shabby and travel-worn. After a seasonable visit, he purchased me a suit of clothes, a railroad ticket to my home and requested the conductor to see me safe to my destination.

I left the train at Lancaster, however, as I had

done before. While in this city I met several half-grown boys who were forming a plan among themselves to run away from their homes and endeavor to enter the Union Army as drummer-boys. As a matter of course, I wanted to join them, not knowing that a ten-year-old boy would be too young to handle an army drum. But the boys refused to accept me as one of their party, and then put me on a freight-train bound for Philadelphia.

One evening, being tired and sleepy from a day's wandering about the city, I climbed upon the platform of a railroad-car, which was standing on Market Street, and soon fell asleep. Shortly after, a policeman came along and aroused me, saying, "My little fellow, I can't allow this."

Learning that I was a little "runaway," and alone at night in the great city, he treated me very kindly, and taking me into a confectionary-store, proceeded to purchase some dainties for me, but I was so badly frightened that I had no desire for food.

After passing the night in a cell, with another occupant, who informed me that he was a furloughed soldier belonging to the Northern Army, one of the officers of the police-station took me to my uncle, who, after giving me some counsel, kept me in the house until my father came for me, he having been instructed of my whereabouts by a despatch from the uncle.

This time I started for home without having an

opportunity to leave the cars at Lancaster, as usual, and on my arrival, I was treated with kindness and consideration by parents and friends. Still, I had not yet seen the world, and I made several other ventures of a similar kind.

On these trips I generally had a hard time, and always ended the journey by arriving at the parental abode about the end of the second week, hungry and sadly dilapidated.

If boys, who have good homes and kind parents, knew what a life of hardship and suffering awaits them, when they leave the comforts of their homes to seek pleasure in traveling, they would think differently of it. No matter where we may go, home is the center toward which our heart will turn.

Boys, stay at home, give up all ideas of roving, and learn a good mechanical trade, or what is much better, go to the country and learn to raise wheat and potatoes. When you have acquired that art, go to the bountiful West, or the "Sunny South," where the Government gives a free farm, of 160 acres of good land, to every applicant.

It has long since been proven that farming is the surest and best road to health, wealth and happiness. The cities are greatly crowded with clerks and professional men who scarcely make a meager living, while the broad, free, beautiful and bounteous country invites all to its bosom.

I suppose the world must have some travelers,

but there are few people who are adapted to endure the hardships and privations of the traveler, who leaves behind him all the comforts and conveniences of home and civilization to accept the accommodations tendered by strangers, or the life he finds in the wilderness.

On one of the latter trips referred to, I went to Philadelphia and the state of Delaware. Reaching Reading, I undertook to do the cooking on a Schuylkill Canal boat until I arrived in Philadelphia. At this city I stepped on board the steamer *Major Reybold* and went to New Castle, Delaware, finally reaching home on foot. On the other journey I proceeded to the city of Baltimore, by way of Chesapeake Bay, after walking fifty miles along the Susquehanna River, to Havre de Grace, at the mouth of the river. After a short stay in this city, I returned by the same route.

One day, while on the wharf at Baltimore, the captain of an English ship, whom I had requested to take me to sea with him, said:

"Go home and tell your mother to bury you, for that will be better for you than a life at sea."

On reaching my home, I attended school until I was fifteen years of age. It seemed to be next to impossible, however, to banish my thirst for travel and adventure; it was a part of my very existence. In daytime my thoughts were of sight-seeing, and at night my dreams were of Indians and their wild, romantic life. But my fondest hopes have been realized, and I now yearn in vain for the happy, peaceful days of my early boyhood.

How precious are the memories of our childhood days, when a dear, loving mother was ever ready and willing to administer to our wants and happiness. Then no heart-pangs and life struggles fell to our lot—all was sweet peace and pleasure.

I sometimes think that when we are surrounded by the selfishness, vanity and avarice of the world, the recollection of our mother and her teachings, are, to a great extent, a safeguard against the evils that surround us, and like a faithful monitor, appeals to our better nature, and tends to raise us above the petty things of earth.

There are few of us who do not, at some time or other during our journey through life, look back upon the joyous, happy spring-time of our existence, with feelings of strangely mingled pleasure and sadness. But taking an active part in the affairs of everyday-life, invariably leads us into channels that allow very little room for the contemplation of bygone-days, or the existence and growth of the finer sentiments of humanity, and we drift into a sphere where the gratification of self is the object ever in view.

I firmly believe that the monster, *selfishness*, is the source of half of all human ills. We are too much in pursuit of our own interests and aims, and give too little thought or attention to the wants and feelings of our fellow beings. In our hurry to gain some coveted goal, we unkindly and thoughtlessly push all others aside, regardless of sensitive natures and generous hearts. What would be considered the height of rudeness and ill-manners in society, or the home-circle, is entirely overlooked in the business arena and the common walks of life.

How genial and consoling is the company of good books. Friends may leave us, the world may seem cold and neglectful, but our books are always the same true, unselfish and interesting companions, whether our communion with them be in the luxurious parlor, the scantily furnished garret, beneath the branches of a drooping willow or riding along in the railway-coach. We can read a book and imagine ourselves having a face to face conversation with its author, for his very heart and mind are portrayed on every page.

CHAPTER II.

Stern winter never comes in that auspicious clime,
The fields are florid with unfading prime;
From the bleak pole no winds inclement blow,
Mould the round hail, or flake the fleecy snow;
But from the Pacific the land inhales
The unceasing murmur of western gales.

ANON.

I LEAVE HOME AGAIN, AND ENTER A PHILADELPHIA LAWYER'S
OFFICE—ON TO CHICAGO—NEWSPAPERS AND THE FIRE—
"HO! FOR CALIFORNIA!"—HOW I TRAVELED AND MADE A
SETTLING-DOWN-FUND AT THE SAME TIME—SAN FRANCISCO
AND ITS PEOPLE—THE EFFECT TRAVELING HAS UPON THE
HEART AND MIND—THE "GOLDEN STATE"—ARROW POINTS
OF THE WAPOO INDIANS—NAPA VALLEY—BUFFALO BILL.

IN the fall of 1869, when in my sixteenth year, I
again left home, more than ever determined to see
something of the world. My first point of destination was Philadelphia, where I obtained a situation as copyist for Edward Waln and W. H. Sut-
ton, lawyers occupying offices on Walnut Street.

After remaining six months I visited the cities of
New York and Albany, and then, after returning to
my home for a short time, I proceeded to Chicago.
Here I secured a good position in the office of the
Chicago Sun, published by H. L. Goodall & Co.

During the burning of Chicago, in October, 1871,

most all the newspaper offices in the city, except
the *Sun* office, were consumed by the flames, and
as news was scarce, there was a great demand for
the remaining papers, which were published almost
in the midst of the ashes. So, with some of the
other office hands, I started out as a news-boy, and
until the other journals made their appearance, I
made some money, as I sold the papers at ten, fifteen, twenty-five and fifty cents a copy.

Shortly after the fire I became restless, and leaving my situation, I went to Pennsylvania. After
visiting my home, I started for Omaha, Nebraska,
stopping at Cincinnati, St. Louis and Kansas City.

At Omaha I secured a pass to California from
the Hon. George Frost, of the Union Pacific Railroad. I remember the genial-hearted gentleman
and his most excellent wife, with profound respect.

During my travels I made it an object to lay by
a small sum of money each week or month, toward
what I termed *my settling-down-fund*, and the exact amount had to be saved, even if I was in need
of a dinner, or a place to lay my head. As I never
learned the use of cards, liquor and tobacco, no
dimes were spent for such things.

When I became weary of the monotony of traveling, I took my place at the printers' type-case until the desire to move on overcame me. Sometimes, when tired of the confinement and tedious-
ness of the printing office, I would try the canvass-

ing business, for I was generally successful at that, and besides, I liked to be in the open air, and get around to see the ladies and the babies.

In this way I managed to see the country and increase my fund at the same time. This is not referred to by way of self-commendation—far from it, for I dislike any sentiment or motive that savors of boasting, show or pride; but as the incident is a part of my narrative I insert it.

I generally managed to get free passage over the railroad and steamboat lines through the kindness and courtesy of the officials and the newspaper fraternity, though at times I was obliged to rough it, and on many occasions I walked hundreds of miles along railroads, and through the interior, having in that way, a far better opportunity of seeing the country than could be obtained by faster travel.

During my travels I held situations on the following newspapers, and I remember the proprietors, and my brother workmen, with kindness and respect:

Star-Vindicator—McAllister, Indian Territory,
Commercial—Chattanooga, Tennessee,
Sun—Wilmington, North Carolina,
Messenger—Petersburg, Virginia,
Union—Jacksonville, Florida,
Mirror—Fernandina, Florida,
Okefenokean—DuPont, Georgia,
Sun—Chicago, Illinois,

Herald—Dixon, Illinois,
Pantagraph—Sioux Falls, Dakota Territory,
Post—Neosho Falls, Kansas,
Herald—Wyandotte, Kansas,
Republican—West Point, Nebraska,
Pioneer—Niobrara, Nebraska,
News—Texarkana, Texas,
Advocate—McKinney, Texas,
Times—Chanute, Kansas,
Republican—Ottawa, Kansas,
Progress—Rock Falls, Illinois,
Independent—Sioux Falls, Dakota Territory,
News Letter—Olathe, Kansas,
Independent—Burlington, Kansas,
Republican—Wahoo, Nebraska,
Journal—Neligh, Nebraska,
Citizen—Bonhomme, Dakota,
Advocate—Huntsville, Alabama,
Courier—Tyler, Texas,
News—Denison, Texas,
Advance—Chetopa, Kansas,
Plaindealer—Garnett, Kansas,
Gazette—Onawa, Iowa,
Fireside Companion—St. Paul, Minnesota,
Journal—Northfield, Minnesota,
Courier—Bristol, Tennessee,
Recorder—Savannah, Georgia,
News—McGregor, Iowa,
News—Duluth, Minnesota.

As I passed over the great Western Plains and the Rocky Mountains, while on my way to California, in the month of November, I saw very little of interest, as the country along the way was clothed in a monotonous mantle of snow and ice; so I pass over the trip without giving it further notice. But elsewhere in the work, will be found a description of a journey across the Continent in summer time.

After visiting Sacramento and San Francisco, I went up to the Calistoga Hot Sulphur Springs, situated sixty miles north of San Francisco, near the Petrified Forest.

San Francicco is situated on a peninsula between the Bay of San Francisco and the Pacific Ocean. It is the largest city and the great commercial conto of the Pacific Coast, and is justly styled the "New-York of the Western Coast." The population of this city includes people from almost every part of the world, the largest foreign element being the Chinese.

The entrance to the harbor is excellent, and is called the "Golden Gate." Vessels and steamers ply between San Francisco and almost every port in the known world.

Sir Francis Drake, an English navigator, visited the Pacific Coast in 1579, and spent several months in the harbor of the Bay of San Francisco. He named the country "New Albion," and claimed it for the British Government. No steps, however, ere ever taken by the English to ratify the claim, and it became a Spanish possession. In 1848 it was acquired by the United States, since which time California, and San Francisco especially, has grown in wealth and commercial importance, to a marvelous extent.

The discovery of gold in California, to which the city of "big bonanza men" owes its existence, was made in 1848, on the American Fork of the Sacramento River, by an American named Marshall, who was employed to build a saw-mill by General Sutter, a Swiss settler.

Great and rich as California is as a gold producing state, the agricultural resources are more valuable, and the shipment of wheat is very large.

The climate of San Francisco is most delightful, snow and ice are unknown, and the flowers never cease to bloom, while during the warmest months, a breeze from the ocean almost constantly passes over the city. There is no winter in the valleys of California, though the mountain tops are covered with snow all the year, and the two seasons are known as "the wet and the dry months."

The people of San Francisco are noted for being fast money-makers, energetic, sociable and generous in the extreme. Many of them crossed the Plains in ox-teams, in the early days of immigration to the "El Dorado," and having suffered hardships and poverty before reaching the golden vein, they have become better and nobler after the trial.

By traveling, a person gains a knowledge of human nature, and of men and things generally, that cannot be obtained so well in any other way. I do not think I "know it all," however. What little I have learned of the world has taught me to place upon self, a depreciation that was once contrary to my disposition. Learning that "one half the world don't know how the other half lives," and that none of us can fully understand or appreciate another's actions and motives, has taught me charity and humility that was once foreign to my nature.

California is noted for its fine fruit and vegetables, as well as for its immense yield of wheat. In the southern part of the state, oranges, lemons and other semi-tropical fruits are produced. The natural scenery of the state is grand, and is not surpassed in any other part of the Union. The Yosemite Valley and Falls, the Big Tree Groves, Hot Sulphur Springs, Petrified Forest and the majestic Sierra Nevada Mountains, are some of the natural wonders of this favored "Golden State."

The scenery at the upper end of Napa Valley is beautiful and romantic. Deep, rocky gorges, in which leap bright, flashing torrents, formed by the melting snow on the far distant mountain tops, or the inexhaustible springs in the hills, are on every hand; beautiful, fragrant flowers bend in the cool breeze that wafts their sweet perfume through the

lovely green valleys; birds of rare plumage warble
their notes among the branches of grand old trees,
and dart from limb to limb, as the tramp of the
hunter beneath, breaks the solitude of the forest.

While hunting in the mountains, near Calistoga,
I found arrow heads that had been made by the
Wapoo Indians out of black lava. They were similar in formation to flint arrow heads, that I have
since found in various parts of the states and territories. Since the Indians can secure iron and steel
for manufacturing their implements, they make very
little use of flint and bone.

Napa Valley lies between two thickly timbered
mountain ridges, and is well watered by numerous
small streams. The valley was originally owned by
the Wapoo Indians, a few of whom still linger on
their once favorite hunting-ground.

After passing a few weeks in California, and having some grand hunts in the forests, I returned to
Pennsylvania. Soon after leaving Ogden, Utah, I
was detained at several points on the Union Pacific
Railroad, by snow blockades, so that I was three
weeks in making the trip.

While I was at North Platte, Nebraska, W. F.
Cody, otherwise known as "Buffalo Bill," was preparing to start for the buffalo range, as a guide for
the Russian Duke Alexis and a party of bordermen.

Mr. Cody is a man of fine personal appearance,
and his countenance indicates him to be a man of

fine organization and generous impulses, and few
people, not knowing his history, would suppose
that quiet, mild-looking man, to be the bold and
fearless hunter and guide he is. Mr. Cody has a
wife, and calls Omaha his home. He is a man of
education and refinement, and has served in the Nebraska Legislature, as well as performed the irk-
some duty of the author; still, he prefers the wild
life of the hunter, trapper and guide.

Missing the train at North Platte, one morning,
I concluded to start out on foot, intending to get
on a train the next day at some station further on.
After following the "iron trail" all day, over an apparently boundless prairie, I reached a "dug-out,"
or under-ground dwelling, near Willow Island, in
the evening.

I had been guided to the place by the light of the
fire glowing out of the chimney. As I approached
the subterranean cabin, I was made aware of my
nearness to it, by striking my head against a dead
deer that had been hung up near the door, but
which I could not see on account of the darkness.

I was kindly received by the six or eight sturdy,
warm-hearted hunters whom I found there, and
supper, consisting of venison, warm biscuit and
coffee, was immediately prepared for me. After
spending a few hours in story-telling, we retired
to a comfortable bed of blankets and robes.

CHAPTER III.

Long years ago, ere my hair turned gray,
  Friends gathered round de ole cabin home,
Happy, contented, we passed de time away,
  But now dey's in Heaven, and beck'ning me to come.

Massa and Missus both sleep on de hill,
  Where little birds their songs love to sing,
Time has done its work, and used de ole place up,
  De weeds are high, de fence is down, and dried up is de spring.
                                        H. DUMARS.

NEW YORK—PHILADELPHIA—I START FOR THE SUNNY SOUTH—
BALTIMORE—WASHINGTON—RICHMOND—THE LIBBY PRISON—
ATLANTA—OLD COLORED "UNCLES" AND "AUNTIES" OF THE
SOUTH—THE PRESENT RELATION BETWEEN FORMER MASTER
AND FORMER SLAVE—A FORTUNE AWAITS THE MAN WHO
WILL INVENT A MACHINE FOR PICKING COTTON—HOW THE
COTTON, RICE, SUGAR, TURPENTINE AND TAR ARE MADE—
MONTGOMERY—MOBILE—HOW THE NORTHERN TRAVELER IS
TREATED BY THE SOUTHERN PEOPLE—NEW ORLEANS.

THE next morning I bid the hunters adieu, and
continued my journey eastward to New York and
Philadelphia, by way of Chicago and Pittsburgh.

New York is the chief city and the greatest commercial metropolis in America. The harbor is one
of the best in the world, and the number of vessels
that arrive annually, is estimated at about twenty
thousand. The masts of the ships are so numerous,
and so close together, that they resemble, at a distance, a forest of branchless trees.

Broadway is probably the handsomest street in the world, and presents a wonderful scene of animation and business. It is six miles in length, and contains a large number of splendid marble and iron buildings. The resident population of the city is over a million, and the number of strangers in the city, on any day, is supposed to be from one to two hundred thousand.

The present site of the city was visited by Henry Hudson, in 1609, and soon afterward, a colony of Dutch went to the place and erected a fort and a few houses, naming the place New Amsterdam.

Philadelphia is, without any exception, the finest and most attractive city in the United States. A very pleasing feature of the "Quaker City" is the beauty and cleanliness of its streets, and the magnificence of its buildings, both public and private. The miles and miles of white marble door-steps, and door and window-sills, found in most all parts of the metropolis, is something not so universally met with in any other city.

At the wharves of the Delaware River, vessels and steamships from almost every known port, can be seen arriving and departing, and present a scene of commotion only to be witnessed at the wharves of a great city. Philadelphia contains many public buildings of 'interest, among which are the State House, in which independence was declared in the year 1776, the Permanent Centennial Buildings, the Mint, Girard College, the Navy Yard, Laurel Hill Cemetery and the Fairmount Park and Water Works, the latter two resorts being situated along the banks of the beautiful Schuylkill River.

The population of the city is nearly one million, and there are more houses in the place than there are in any other city in the Union. Philadelphia is the greatest manufacturing city in America, there being about ten thousand manufactories. The city was laid out by William Penn, in 1682, from whom it received its name, which means "brotherly love."

Upon reaching Philadelphia, on my trip from the West, I obtained a clerkship in a store, where I remained several months, and then started on a tour through the Southern States.

Baltimore was the first objective point. This is sometimes called the "Monumental City," as it contains a large number of fine memorial works of art. The place has much the air and appearance of a Southern city. The people are polite and courteous, refined and hospitable, and loud in the praise of their beautiful city.

The shipping and other commercial interests of Baltimore are extensive. Much of the Lake Superior copper is used here. The manufacturing interests of the city are large.

In due time I reached Washington, the city of "magnificent distances," as well as of delightful little parks, or squares, that are almost constantly,

during pleasant weather, thronged with a grand
and lavish display of wealth and luxury.   Yet there
is no other city in the Union where the contrast
between the rich and the poor is so marked as it is
in Washington.   The home of the humble work-
man, in many instances, is but a few squares from
the princely apartments of the portly senator, and
almost within a stone's cast of the great Capitol
Building, are old and dilapidated frame shanties,
the abode of poverty and suffering.

Washington, like Baltimore, contains a large colored population, some of whom are well educated
and in comfortable circumstances, while their less
fortunate brethren live in want and ignorance, but
they are blessed with a fair portion of cheerfulness,
which is a leading trait in the character of the race.

After leaving Baltimore and Washington, the
traveler going south, at once becomes aware of a
marked change in the appearance of the country.
Red sandy soil and pine timber here predominate.
As he passes Alexandria and proceeds on to Richmond, he finds the country presents about the same
general aspect.

Richmond, the capi a'. of Virginia, is finely situated on the James River, and owing to its location,
it somewhat resembles Kansas City or St. Paul. It
contains numerous flour mills and tobacco factories.

While in Richmond I visited the famous Libby
Prison, situated at the corner of Nineteenth and

Cary Streets, where so many Northern prisoners were confined during the late war. The place is now occupied by Libby & Son, as a tobacco house.

The ceiling, walls, floor and window-sills, were covered with the names of the prisoners, and the dates of their capture, written with lead-pencils and carved with pen-knives.

Leaving Richmond, I continued southward, and passed through the staid old towns of Charlotte, Columbia and Augusta. The private dwellings of these cities are generally embowered in orchards, groves of magnolia and other semi-tropical trees, lawns and tastefully arranged flower gardens, which is a beautiful and characteristic feature of Southern towns and cities.

Atlanta, the capital of Georgia, is next reached. This city has grown wonderfully since the war, and has much the spirit and energy of a Western town. It is an important railroad center, and is noted for its iron works and other industries.

One day, while near West Point, Alabama, I met a venerable old colored woman as I was walking toward the town, and being pleased with her good-natured, sunny face, I concluded to have a chat with her. Upon addressing her kindly as, "aunty," a broad smile illuminated her aged face, and she exclaimed somewhat as follows:

"De Lor' bress you honey! I 'spects you's a gemman from de Norf. Dis ole black woman aint got edicashum, but she knows a man what comes from 'Yankeedom' de berry minute her ole eyes see de chile."

There are thousands of old colored "uncles" and "aunties" all through the South, who, having been the faithful servants and companions of "massa" and "missus" for many years, still linger about "de ole plantation," and generally being kindly provided for by their former owners, are now passing their declining days in comparative ease. Being too old to assist in the cotton-field or rice-patch, they linger about the old home that sheltered them before the days of freedom.

Some Northern people entertain the idea that the Southerners have a deep and bitter animosity for the colored freedmen, but that, to a great extent, is an error. It is both beautiful and affecting to see the friendship and respect that exists between the former master and the former slave when a meeting takes place. No matter how far "Uncle Ben" or "Aunt Dinah" may roam, now that they are free, they will return to see "de ole place," and to pay "der 'spects to de white folks."

Still, after all, I have no hesitancy in asserting, that much as I love the South and its people, I dislike slavery, and deem the *principle* to be wrong.

Cotton is the leading product of the South, but South Carolina, Georgia, Alabama and Mississippi, produce the most. When the seed becomes ripe the pods open, and the beautiful snow-white cotton appears. In the fall it is picked—a labor performed entirely by hand, as no machine for picking cotton has ever been invented, and a limitless fortune awaits the man who will produce the machine.

There surely is, somewhere, an ingenious Yankee with brains enough to construct the required instrument, for which service he would be laden with the gratitude, honors and dollars of his Southern brethren.

Lines of merry colored people, male and female, glide between the rows of plants and crowd the fleecy product into bags carried for the purpose. It is afterward put into large baskets and conveyed to the cotton-gin. When the cotton comes from the pod it is mixed with the seed, but a machine for separating them was invented over a hundred years ago by a Yankee named Eli Whitney.

In shape and color, rice resembles wheat, but it requires a low, wet soil. When first planted, it is covered with water, but after it takes root, it must be kept dry. The fields are traversed by small canals, from which the rice-patch can be overflowed in a short time. It requires a large capital and much care, to reap a good crop of rice.

Sugar-cane is cultivated extensively in the states of Louisiana, Mississippi, Alabama and Florida. When the cane is fit to cut, it is stripped of the tops and leaves, cut into short pieces, tied into bundles and carried to the mill. The cane is then crushed between iron rollers, and the juice which is secured, is boiled until it becomes syrup. It is then stirred in coolers until it forms into grains, when it is put into casks having holes in the bottom, and left to drain into large tanks. What remains in the hogshead is brown sugar, and what drips into the tank is molasses.

Turpentine is the sap of the pine tree, and is obtained by cutting a small cavity, called a box, into the trunk of the tree. This is done in the winter, or wet season, and in the spring the sap begins to flow into the box. It next undergoes a distilling process, and after being barrelled, it is ready for the market.

In the production of tar, a cave is made in the earth and filled with pine wood, this next being covered with ground, in order to keep out the air. The wood is then fired, and the sap of the pine runs into a huge pan at the bottom of the cave and becomes tar. Rosin is extracted from turpentine in a crude state.

Montgomery, Alabama, has somewhat the appearance of Albany, New York, on account of its high location. It is the capital of the great cotton state, and is finely located on the Alabama River.

Mobile is situated on a bay, thirty-five miles up from the Gulf of Mexico. It is probably next to New Orleans as a commercial and shipping point.

To use an expression quite common throughout the South, "cotton is king" in Mobile, and the majority of the male residents are interested in the staple, either directly or indirectly.

Here reside some of the "merchant princes" of this "sunny clime," and the enchanting villas and grand mansions of the city are occupied by men who owe their wealth to the cotton-plant.

Mobile, like Charleston and Savannah, is noted for the hospitality and courteous demeanor of its inhabitants.

The suburbs of the city are charming, and the avenues are lined with fine retired residences, surrounded with clusters of beautiful orange and live-oak trees, which abound in this locality.

The city does an immense shipping trade with Northern and European sea-ports, and regular lines of steamers run to Cedar Keys, New Orleans and other points. A large number of sailing craft also ply between Mobile and Appalachicola, St. Marks and other local gulf ports.

I freely assert, as I think all observing Northern men will, who travel through the South, that the inhabitants of this "land of perpetual sunshine and flowers" are as warm-hearted, generous and courteous, as any people in this wide world.

On my way to New Orleans from Mobile, I passed over a railroad running through a large swamp, and the alligators and serpents were ever present.

New Orleans is the great commercial mart of the South, and is a bee-hive of industry. Its shipping trade with all parts of the world ranks next to that of Boston, New York, Philadelphia or Baltimore. The great New Orleans Levee, from which millions of dollar's worth of cotton, sugar, rice and molasses is annually shipped to "Yankeedom" and foreign countries, presents a scene of life and confusion that exists, perhaps, no where else.

It is unlike Northern cities in many respects, as indeed, are all Southern towns. The most notice-able difference in New Orleans being the foreign appearance and customs of many of the residents, who are the descendants of the French settlers.

In the country around New Orleans are grand and luxurious villas. the homes of princely planters, where Southern wealth and refinement are fully represented. Surrounded by live-oak, magnolia, orange, lemon and banana trees, is the mansion of the man counting the annual profit of his sugar plantations by thousands of dollars.

CHAPTER IV.

Across the prairies toward the west,
  We rode at day's declining ;
What radiant pictures we beheld,
  In heavenly ether shining !

Sweet stars above, sweet flowers beneath,
  Shine in the twilight faintly,
While rising in the dusky east,
  The moon grows white and saintly.
                  MARGARET S. SIBLEY.

WALKING ACROSS A TRESTLE BRIDGE AT NIGHT WITH SNAKES AND ALLIGATORS FOR COMPANIONS—THE COLORED PEOPLE OF THE SOUTH—THEIR COMIC PHRASES—ST. LOUIS—THE WESTERN PRAIRIES—A GORGEOUS SCENE—REFLECTIONS— THE AGONY OF THIRST—THE BUFFALO AT HOME—KANSAS.

LEAVING New Orleans, I moved north, shaping my course toward St. Louis. I left the city one evening and walked to a point about eight miles distant, where I expected to meet a train going to Jackson, Mississippi.

The railroad, for part of the way, was built upon low piles through a large swamp, and as I stepped from tie to tie, in the darkness, huge serpents and alligators would leap from the trestle into the water beneath, the splashing as they reached the water, adding greatly to my already uncomfortable frame of mind. Sometimes I would approach within a

few feet of the reptiles before they would spring
into the water, and owing to the darkness, I could
not see them until I approached close to them.

On my way up to St. Louis I passed through
Jackson, Grenada and Water Valley, going by rail-
road, and crossing the Mississippi at Columbus,
Kentucky, into the state of Missouri.

The country adjacent to the Mississippi River,
lying between New Orleans and St. Louis, is more
level and marshy than other sections of the South,
but the other characteristics of both the country
and people, correspond with the general features.

Bread, whether made of wheat flour or corn-meal,
is generally eaten warm, and cold bread or biscuit
is seldom placed upon the table. A great deal of
corn-meal is used by both the rich and the poor, it
being prepared in the shape of hominy, grits, hoe-
cake and pone.

The colored people are healthy and robust, and
are ever happy and cheerful. So long as they have
a pound of bacon and a peck of corn-meal in the
cabin, they are contented, and strangers to "dull
care." These people are very fond of coffee, and
when their financial resources are low, they substitute various ingredients. Among them is parched
corn ground like coffee, or the corn-meal browned;
this is really a better substitute than might be
supposed. A good old colored "aunty," in Georgia,
once made me a cup of corn-coffee, and I must say

that it was, in her language, "right smart coffee."

The colored people have a peculiarity of speech that is truly amusing, and I quote a few phrases for the reader:

"Massa, lemme toat dat package? I's done gone and done it! Pass on dar, nigga, dat chicken got de epizudom! Lookey heah, honey, don't pester dis chile, 'cause I fling you over de fence, shuah!"

St. Louis, situated on the Mississippi twenty-one miles below the mouth of the Missouri, is in several respects a singular place. The people have much the manner and appearance of Southerners, while the city itself resembles Philadelphia in the names and location of the streets; and the iron-works give some parts of the city no small semblance to the black and smoky city of Pittsburgh.

In size and importance St. Louis ranks above Cincinnati and next to Chicago. It is the largest inland steamboat port in the world. It is in direct river communication with New Orleans, Memphis, Pittsburgh, Cincinnati, Kansas City, St. Paul, Omaha and Sioux City, as well as with the forts and Indian agencies on the Upper Missouri.

From St. Louis I proceeded to Wamego, Kansas, by the way of Kansas City, Lawrence and Topeka. Between Wamego and Ellsworth, a point further west, I beheld, for the first time in summer, the mighty Western Prairies in all their gorgeous splendor. It was a lovely, a grand sight, and one to fill

the heart and mind with sentiments and thoughts
far above the strife and contentions of the crowded
districts, where wealth, dress and honors leave so
little time and room for purer thoughts and aims,
and for the enjoyment of the beauties of Nature.

As far as the eye could reach, on every hand, was
the level prairie, relieved occasionally by enchanting little valleys intersected by graceful slopes and
ridges of conical-shaped mounds, covered with tall,
waving grass and prairie flowers. Millions of acres
were thus adorned with beautiful wild flowers and
blossoms of almost every shade and color, which
covered the earth with a mantle of variegated hues.
The heavens were singularly clear, and objects on
the prairie could be seen at a remarkable distance.
Belts and fringes of cottonwood and willow, marked
the course of winding streams, that gave life and
vigor to the vegetation around.

Notwithstanding the trials and disappointments
we suffer here, the world has some pleasures and
attractions for all of us, and we have much to be
thankful for. God gives us beauty and grandeur
of mountain, plain and sea, and seemingly, from the
rippling water, the singing birds and the blooming
flowers, comes a voice of love and cheer, that tends
to soothe the grieving soul and rouse its slumber-
ing energies to renewed activity.

Missing the train at Ellis, Kansas, I started for
Park's Fort on foot, as I had been informed that

the distance was but three miles. After traveling for some time under a scorching hot sun, I found that I had been deceived in the distance to the fort.

Soon I experienced the parching sensation of thirst, so dreaded by the traveler on the plains. The railroad, the Kansas Pacific, here traverses a dry, barren plain known as the American Desert. It is utterly destitute of water, the nearest stream being the Smoky Hill River, twelve miles distant. Even this is merely a brook, which at this point, is so narrow that a horse could leap across it.

I had walked about ten miles when the intense heat, and the suffering brought on by thirst, made me very faint. As I looked over the broad expanse of barren waste on all sides of me, I became much discouraged. Not a single human habitation could be seen, and the only living object within the scope of my vision, was a few straggling herds of antelope and villages of prairie dogs.

That strange, death-like calm, so peculiar to the plains, prevailed over all, making my situation still more desolate. This, with my dreary surroundings, served to increase my misery, and the two iron rails glittering in their sandy bed, reminded me most vividly of civilization.

Upon reaching each successive elevation that lay in my course, I hoped to see the fort, but nothing but a vast tract of dry, sterile table-land met my eager gaze. My suffering increased at every step, and finally I started to the river for water, not thinking that I might never reach it in my exhausted condition.

After walking about a mile, I abandoned the undertaking, and returned to the railroad. I was now nearly overcome with thirst and heat; my tongue was parched and swollen, my eyes were dim and painful, and an inward burning heat seemed to be consuming me. I became confused, and found that my mind, as well as my body, was overpowered by the agony of thirst.

On reaching a large pile of railroad-ties, near the track, I climbed upon it to look once more for an evidence of water, but nothing but long ridges of dark, barren bluffs and dry, sandy ravines, wrapped in the dim screen of smoky haze, met my view; and the false, fascinating mirage, delineating imaginary streams of rippling water, mocked my failing eyes.

In a fit of despair I sank to the ground, concluding that there I must die. I lay on the shady side of the ties, with face downward, thinking to prolong life by the earth's moisture. This is the last resort of plainsmen when suffering for water.

Objects around me were no longer plainly visible, and I felt that I was fast falling a prey to that indescribable stupor, that knows no waking, when occasioned by the pangs of thirst.

Finally, arousing from the lethargy into which I had fallen, I made another effort to reach the river, but in vain. I passed several buffalo-wallows and ravines on the way, but not a drop of water could I find. The ground, in some places, was strewn with dead buffaloes that had been killed merely for their hides, and I searched the decaying carcasses in vain, for a drop of blood or moisture to quench the burning flame within me.

At last, I fancied that I noticed some object in the distance, but my mind and eyes were so effected, that I doubted the reality of it, at first; but as I proceeded toward it, urged onward by the hope of finding water, I could discern two horses, and next a wagon containing two men.

I felt confident that the wagon contained some water, and with renewed effort I started toward it. My feelings upon receiving an answer in the affirmative, to my inquiry for water, cannot well be portrayed. At first, I was too weak and nerveless to hold the water-keg that was handed to me, but by degrees, my strength returned somewhat, and then I found relief from the terrible pangs of thirst.

My benefactors proved to be buffalo hunters, on their way to Ellis with a load of hides. After resting awhile, I started for Park's Fort, which was the first station west of Ellis, and twenty miles distant instead of three, as I had been informed before I started out from the latter place.

In a short time after leaving the hunters, the west-bound express train came along, and signaling for the engineer to stop, I stepped on board and rode to the fort.

To this day, I seldom pass a stream of water or a spring, without recalling my experience on the American Desert. A bright, sparkling river, creek or rivulet, is now, to my eyes, one of the most enchanting objects of Nature.

I remained a few days with the soldiers at Park's Fort, and then went to Denver, Colorado.

I was now in the buffalo range of Kansas, and as I rode along on the cars, the shaggy monsters were roaming over the prairie in glorious freedom. This was in the summer of 1872, and the buffaloes were not so plenty as they had been a few years previous, when the railroad was first completed; then they were so numerous that the trains had to be stopped in order to let the animals cross the track.

In referring to the American Desert, in western Kansas, I would not lead the reader to suppose that the whole state is a barren waste—far from it. Kansas is one of the garden states of the West, but there is a narrow district, extending from southern Nebraska, through western Kansas, to the Indian Territory, that is so destitute of vegetation and water, and so productive of sandy plains and beds of alkali, that it has received the appellation of the American Desert.

CHAPTER V.

Oh, a boundless realm is the mighty West!
A realm that a king might sigh for,—
With its precious gold, and its silver white,
And its prairies broad, and mirages bright;
'Tis a land we well might hie for!

What mountains tower in the peerless West,
High up in the azure sky-lands!
Their brows bedecked with the virgin snow,
They gaze afar o'er the plains below—
O'er forests, lakes and highlands.

What pathless woods in the lordly West
Reach forth from her cloud-capped mountains!
How grand are her turbulent inland seas
Whose billows roll in the stormy breeze—
Lured out from their mystic fountains!

THOS. L. SMITH.

DENVER CITY—SCENERY IN THE ROCKY MOUNTAINS—STARVING
SOLDIERS EATING THEIR MULES—GRASSHOPPERS—THE ECHO
CANYON—OLD MORMON BATTLEMENTS—THE ONE THOUSAND
MILE TREE—SALT LAKE CITY—A PRINTING OFFICE ON THE
MARCH—BRIGHAM YOUNG—THE UTAH SULPHUR SPRINGS—
THE NEVADA DESERT—HUMBOLDT WELLS—SCENES IN THE
SIERRA NEVADA MOUNTAINS—SNOW SHEDS—THE CAUTION
OF THE INDIANS—THE OLD PAIUTE—THE GREAT SALT
LAKE—IN CLOSE QUARTERS WITH THE PAWNEE INDIANS—
A LIST OF MY INDIAN CURIOSITIES AND OTHER RELICS.

DENVER, the capital of Colorado, is a handsome
young city, and has had a wonderful growth. It is
finely situated on the plains, twelve miles from the
foot of the Rocky Mountains, whose snow-capped
peaks rise grandly among the fleecy clouds, and like

grim sentinels, seem to guard the city. Denver is
the great center of trade for the mining and stock-
raising districts of Colorado and New Mexico.

After spending a few days in this "City of the
Plains," I visited Golden City, situated fourteen
miles distant, in the mountains. I then returned
to Denver and started for the Pacific Coast, by way
of Greely, Cheyenne and Salt Lake City.

The lover of Nature finds ample material for admiration and thought, while traveling over the great
Union Pacific Railroad, between Cheyenne and Ogden. One continuous scene of mountain chains,
rugged ravines, mighty torrents and cataracts, arid
wastes and alkaline deserts, relieved, at intervals,
by lovely little valleys, through whose bosom flow
streams of cool, sparkling water, continually meets
the eye on every hand.

North of the railroad, tower the Black Hills, and
south of it, is the most massive range of the Rocky
Mountains. Sherman is the summit-level of the
railroad, and the highest point in America, or perhaps in the world, reached by the locomotive.

Great mountains of rock, whose grim and ever
shadowy outlines seem to portray traces of temple,
spire and pyramid, the weird grandeur of which is
most marvelous and striking, is to be seen at every
turn. Many of these rocks consist of red sandstone,
and fancy sees them showing the sculptor's magic
handicraft.

At Fort Bridger, before the existence of the railroad, three regiments of United States troops, who
had been sent out to fight the Mormons, in 1857,
endured terrible suffering. Closed in on all sides
by the deep winter snows, in the very heart of the
bleak mountains, and the wagon supply-train captured by the enemy, they were obliged to kill and
eat their mules; even the skins of the mules were
eaten by the starving soldiers. Many died from
hunger and cold, as no food from the East reached
them until the close of the following summer.

This section of the West is still inhabited by the
Snake, or Shoshonee Indians, and groups of them
often make their appearance on some neighboring
ridge or spur of the mountains, and watch the puffing "iron-horse" as it dashes through the mountain
solitude and proclaims to the red man, that, "Westward the star of empire takes its way," regardless
of the rights, feelings and interests of the much
abused Indians.

The chief of the Shoshonee Indians is Washakie,
a man much respected by Western people who can
appreciate a truly "good Indian." In the character of this fine old chief are beautifully blended the
traits of truth and honesty. He has not been on
the war-path against the whites for years, but in
the summer of 1879 a part of his tribe was hostile,
and killed a number of settlers, carried women into
captivity, destroyed houses, stock, etc.

Some places in Wyoming the grasshoppers are so plenty that when they settle upon the ground, the traveler finds walking very unpleasant and fatiguing, as the shoes become slippery from crushing the insects. A person who has never seen a large swarm of grasshoppers in the West, can have but a faint idea of their number, or the injury they can inflict upon vegetation. They often descend in a heavy, blinding shower, and their number is so immense that they darken the sun like a cloud.

Echo Canyon, on the line of the Union Pacific Railroad, is one of the most sublime sights in North America. It is a deep, precipitous cavity, seven or more miles in length, and half a mile wide. On one side it is bordered by high, rocky cliffs, hundreds of feet in height, worn into numerous fancy and grotesque shapes by the rushing water, while on the other side it is closed in by a chain of bluffs. In the deep ravine thus formed, flows a mighty, dashing stream.

In some places, vast piles of granite and boulder cause the channel to break, and half-way down the canyon, the stream becomes quite narrow, but much stronger and more rapid, while the banks, or rather walls, are more precipitous. The rocky embankments here form many fantastic outlines, which in the dark shadows of the mountains, imagination can picture to be almost any object.

Near the end of the canyon, on the mountains,

ten hundred feet above the valley, are the remains of
a fort which the followers of Brigham Young built
when the United States troops were pursuing them.
Here the Mormons threw down upon the heads of
their pursuers, rocks and stones which they had
collected for the purpose.

A few miles from Echo Canyon, at a place called
the Narrows, is a solitary pine tree on the bank of
a stream. No other tree is near it, and what gives
it a name and notice, is the singular fact that it is
just one thousand miles from the Missouri River.
Upon the tree is a board bearing this inscription:
"One Thousand Mile Tree."

In this vicinity there are several curious freaks of
nature to be seen in the rocky masses, known as
Pulpit Rock, Witches' Rocks, Gate and the Slide.
All are wild looking and weird, and their singular
and uncouth appearance in the gloomy wilds, fills
the traveler with feelings of awe and solemnity.

Continuing westward, I reached Ogden and Salt
Lake City. These towns were laid out with good
taste and judgment by the Mormons, and they are
beautiful and interesting.

According to the statement of the late Brigham
Young, the site of Salt Lake City was first seen by
him in a dream. When he entered the Salt Lake
Basin, he found a stream of fresh water bubbling
up from the earth, and he at once named it "City
Creek." He then commenced the building of Salt

Lake City, which is situated in one of the grandest
and most picturesque sections of the Far West.

The Mormons carried a printing-office with them
across the plains, when they moved from Nauvoo,
Illinois, to the wilds of Utah, and a newspaper was
published on the march, the edition being dropped
along the way for the emigrants of the caravan.

Of course, there were a great many discouraged
and weary people in the party who needed the aid
and stimulating influence of printer's ink to revive
them; and the valor, skill and fortitude of the editors and printers, who under such overwhelming
difficulties, "got out the paper," deserve the admiration of all.

The Mormon metropolis is situated near the foot
of the Wahsatch Mountains, the ever snow-covered
peaks of which, furnish much of the water that flows
through the streets of the city. These streams are
pure and cool, and flow on each side of the streets,
keeping the locust shade trees in beautiful foliage
during the hot summer months.

The private residences are of almost every imaginable style, and surrounded by orchards and fine
gardens. Many of the houses, especially those built
during the early days of the settlement, consist of
adobe. The city covers an area of eight or more
square miles, and contains a population of about
twenty thousand.

The late home of the Mormon leader stands in

from the street, a short distance, and is quite an imposing structure. The gardens around it are handsomely laid out, and carefully cultivated.

Brigham Young was a good-looking old man, and retained his vigor of body and mind almost to his last days. He died at the advanced age of eighty years. In appearance, he was stout and robust, his eyes were mild and drowsy looking, and the expression of his compressed lips denoted good-nature, rather than firmness; he wore no beard except short chin-whiskers extending to the ear. He had more the appearance of an unassuming, honest farmer, than a great financier, a marvelous manager and the husband of nineteen wives.

After spending three weeks in Salt Lake City, I started for California, traveling over the Utah Central and the Central Pacific Railroads.

Sunset on the Great Salt Lake is a grand sight; rich and gorgeous is the coloring of mountain-peak, rocky canyon and placid lake, when they are all enveloped in "the dying halo of departing day." The heart swells with admiration as the traveler stands and views these enduring evidences of a living God in his works.

The air from the lake is pure, cool and invigorating, and silence reigns over all; not a sound mars the solemn calm as the mellow light of the moon tinges the peaceful lake, and illuminating the dark mountain, presents a scene that pen cannot picture.

Between Salt Lake City and Ogden, a few miles
from the lake, are several hot sulphur springs. A
very unpleasant sulphurous odor proceeds from
them, though they are said to contain rare medical
properties. The temperature of the springs is 102
degrees, Fahrenheit.

Much of the country in Nevada, traversed by the
Central Pacific Railroad, is supposed by geologists,
to have been, at a remote period of time, the bed
of a great sea. The utter desolation and barrenness
of the section can scarcely be imagined; in some
places, the ground is so thickly covered with alkali,
that at first sight, especially at a distance, the substance is often supposed to be lime or snow.

Water is exceedingly scarce, and what little does
exist, is found in natural wells in the bottom of
deep ravines. Among these, the Humboldt Wells
are the largest. There are about twenty of them,
situated in a little valley which they water. These
wells are very deep, and are believed to be the cra-
ters of extinct volcanoes.

At nearly every station on the line of the road,
between Ogden and San Francisco, Indians of the
Shoshonee, Ute, Pahute, Digger and other tribes
made their appearance, gaudily painted and ornamented. These Indians subsist principally upon
small game and roots, though at times, they move
north, into Idaho and Montana, where they hunt
mountain-sheep, bears, deer and other game.

At Truckee, California, a grand view of the Sierra Nevada Mountains is obtained. The wild, shaggy and towering summits are covered with snow every month in the year, and contrast vividly with the deep blue sky which they seem to touch. The mountain sides are crowned with grand old pines of at least a century's growth.

The valleys and dells are beautiful and romantic, and most every one contains a glittering stream, which, continually leaping over the craggy rocks, casts it pearly spray on every side, and fills the forest and glens with wild, unceasing prattle.

There are some beautiful fresh water lakes in this vicinity, among the largest of which are the Lakes Tahoe and Donner. The water is clear as crystal, and very deep, and affords an abundance of fish.

Between the summit of the mountains and the city of Sacramento, the railroad traverses a succession of tunnels and snow-sheds, so close together, that for miles, they appear like one tunnel or shed. There are over fifty miles of snow-sheds, and they are very necessary, for some places in the mountains, the snow falls to a depth of fifteen feet, but between the western base of the mountains and the Pacific Ocean, winter is unknown.

The plan of connecting the Atlantic and Pacific Oceans by a railroad, was first suggested to the American people by Asa Whitney, of New York. At a meeting held in Philadelphia, in 1846, numerous projects for executing the great enterprise were formed. It was not, however, until 1863 that a company was organized, and in the following year, the first ground was broken.

On the 10th of May, 1869, the track-layers of the Union and Central Pacific Railroads met, and formed a junction near the head of the Great Salt Lake, thus completing a continuous iron band from New-York to San Francisco.

After visiting Sacramento, Oakland and San Francisco, I shaped my course eastward. The desire to travel ever kept me moving. Leaving Sacramento one morning, on foot, I walked to a point about fifty miles distant. I traveled nearly all of the following night through the mountains, and toward morning, foot-sore and weary, I lay down in an old hut, near the railroad, and fell asleep.

At various places on the way, during the night, I saw the camp-fires of Indians, who were fishing in the mountain streams, but I did not go to them for food or shelter, fearing to wander over rocks and torrents in the darkness of night.

Near Truckee, I visited a camp of Washoe Indians. I purchased a string of shell-beads from an old warrior whom I met in the camp, but both he and his wife gave me to understand that they had such a poor opinion of a white man's honesty, that I would have to place the money in their hands before they would part with the beads.

On the Humboldt River, near Winnemucca, in
Nevada, I entered a village of Pahute Indians, and
was kindly received by them. I was sociably entertained in the lodge of an old, scar-covered chief,
who graciously showed me his implements of war
and the chase, also a fine collection of furs.

Near Monument Rock, in Utah, on my way to the
East, I took a bath in Great Salt Lake. The surface of the lake, near the shore, is covered with
dead insects, and the shore is lined with pure crystallized salt, formed by the evaporation of the water
that dashes upon the beach.

The water is dark and sluggish, and destitute of
fish or any living thing, but a species of sea-gull
inhabits its surface. The lake is so strongly impregnated with salt, that the motion of the bather
causes the salt to rise from the bottom, where the
water is shallow, and upon emerging from the lake,
he is surprised to find pure, white salt in his hair,
ears, nose and eyes.

It is said that in this lake a live human body cannot sink, and I know by personal experience, that
some peculiarity of the water prevents the bather
from remaining beneath the surface. Nine barrels
of this water evaporated, will produce one barrel of
pure salt. Where water is drained off of shallow
inlets of the lake, the crystallized salt is often found
in vast beds, two and three inches in depth. In the
year 1877, the firm of Lawrence & Burgess, who

have a salt manufactory on the lake shore, produced 1,000 tons of salt by evaporation.

Ogden, Utah, is the junction of the Union and Central Pacific Railroads, and is situated thirty-six miles north of Salt Lake City, which it somewhat resembles in general characteristics.

Between North Platte and Grand Island, in Nebraska, by permission of the fireman, I rode on the front part of a locomotive. It was a lovely summer night, and all Nature seemed wrapped in slumber as the huge, fiery monster dashed through the wild prairie solitudes like a thing of life, arousing the timid antelope, the watchful wolf and the yelping coyote from their lair in the tall, rank grass.

Several miles south of Grand Island, I visited a village of Pawnee Indians, situated on the Platte River. At that time, the summer of 1872, these Indians had a good buffalo range, were very independent and quite troublesome to the settlers in western Nebraska, frequently killing ranchmen and herders, driving off stock, etc.

When I entered their camp they were very rude, and soon began to search my pockets, and make themselves otherwise unpleasantly familiar. They then led me into a lodge full of armed and painted warriors, where I was searched again. I began to get uneasy, and arose to leave the wigwam, but an Indian compelled me to sit down again. He then tried to take my revolver, but I repulsed him, and retained it in my hand with the muzzle toward him.

They crowded around me still closer, and one young brave came in and stood by my side with a glittering tomahawk in his hand. At this juncture, an old gray-headed warrior entered the lodge in a hasty manner, and addressing me with the usual Indian salute of "How! How!" led me out from the presence of the other Indians. Then, with a smile indicating friendship and protection, he conducted me to his lodge, where I was safe from further molestation or danger.

In my experience with the Indians, I generally found warm friends among the old men and women, when the younger people were selfish and hostile. They would give me the best accommodations their lodges afforded, call me their son and urge me to remain with them always. I also made it an object to become on terms of friendship with the young children, and thus won the confidence and respect of their parents. Among the Yankton Sioux and Spotted Tail's tribe of Brule Sioux, were some little boys and girls to whom I became much attached, and I passed some pleasant hours amusing and instructing them.

After a short stay in camp, during which I visited different tents, and saw the Indians at their various occupations of pounding corn, dressing hides and preparing food, I returned to the railroad.

Upon reaching Omaha I went up to Sioux City,

and from there I started for Yankton, Dakota, on foot, there being no railroad to Yankton at that time. My route lay over a beautiful prairie district of Southern Dakota, between the Missouri River on the south, and a chain of huge, treeless bluffs on the north.

About ten miles from Yankton I was overtaken by a rain-storm, and not being near shelter at the time, I was obliged to face it. In an hour or more, however, I came in sight of a house about a mile distant. Hungry, weary and wet to the skin, I was urged onward by the hope of shelter and a warm supper, and I was not disappointed.

Upon reaching the house, I was met at the door by a Miss Jennie Hayes, a bright, handsome young lady, who comprehending my condition at a glance, invited me into the house at once, and removing my wet coat, she immediately supplied a dry one of her father's in its place.

After tea, I naturally wondered what was to become of me; the rain was still falling in torrents, and the thought of continuing my journey was not pleasant. As the men were in Yankton on business, I could scarcely expect to remain over night, but my kind young hostess and her good mother, divining my thoughts, relieved my mind in this wise: "You must not think of going further to-night, and we will endeavor to make you comfortable," they said. So the affair was arranged, satisfactory to all.

During my travels and residence among the various Indian tribes, I collected a number of their implements of war, the chase and domestic use, a portion of which I still retain, and append the list for the perusal of the reader.

On several occasions I was engaged by Professor S. S. Haldeman, of Chickies, Pennsylvania, to make expeditions through the Southern States for the purpose of opening ancient Indian mounds; I also traveled among the Sioux Indians in Dakota, and the Chippewas of the Upper Mississippi, purchasing for him stone implements, in occasional use by the Western Indians. A description of these journeys is given elsewhere in the work.

Mr. Haldeman has one of the finest and most valuable individual collections of Indian antiquities in existence; many of his objects being superior to those of the National Collection at Washington.

The Professor has devoted more than fifty years to the study and research of the antiquities of the North American Indians, and being a wealthy man with a liberal hand, he has spent money in the cause without flinching. His collection is designed to be a gift to the Academy of Natural Sciences, in Philadelphia, but all duplicates will be distributed among other institutions.

The following objects are only those which I find in my own collection, what I secured for Mr. S. S. Haldeman are not mentioned.

Leggins—Brule squaw, Ponca River, Dakota.
Stone pipe—Sioux, Missouri River, Dakota.
Shot pouch—Chippewa, Northeastern Dakota.
Indian rope—Santee Sioux, Southern Dakota.
Glass beads—Shoshonee, near Ogden, Utah.
Iron arrow-points—Sioux, Cheyenne River, Dakota.
Horn spoon—Ponca, Niobrara River, Dakota.
Flint-tipped arrow—Sioux, Ponca River, Dakota.
Knife sheath—Chippewa, Northern Minnesota.
Stone pipe—Ponca, Missouri River, Dakota.
Shell beads—Washoe, near Truckee, California.
Iron arrow-heads—Pawnee, Central Nebraska.
Snow shoe—Chippewa, Northern Minnesota.
Shell beads—Sioux squaw, Cheyenne River, Dakota.
Stone pipe—Brule Sioux, Ponca River, Dakota.
Indian hair—Pahute, Humboldt River, Nevada.
Ear ornaments—Sioux, Cheyenne River, Dakota.
Ornamented rawhide—Arickaree, North Dakota.
Iron tomahawk—Ponca, Missouri River, Dakota.
Moccasins—Sioux squaw, Ponca River, Dakota.
Stone pipe—Chippewa, Northern Minnesota.
Hunting knife—Arickaree squaw, North Dakota.
Neck ornament—Sioux, Missouri River, Dakota.
Black lava arrow-heads—Calistoga, California.
Indian pottery etc.—M. Burney's Forest, Florida.
Ornamented birch-bark—Chippewa, Minnesota.
Stone war-club—Sioux, Ponca River, Dakota.
Bow and arrows—Sioux, Missouri River, Dakota.
Stone hoe—Mr. J. Wiley, Bainbridge, Pennsylvania.

Flint arrow-heads, stone tomahawk, chisels, knife,
borers, corn pestles, polishing stone, scraper—
ancient Indian village sites and fishing camps on
the Susquehanna River; presented by Mr. Jacob
L. Stehman, of Bainbridge, Pennsylvania.

Indian pottery, stone tomahawk and pipe-stems—
Mr. J. H. Wittmer, Washington, Pennsylvania.

Stone tomahawk—Columbia, Pennsylvania.

Mormon relics—Salt Lake City, Utah.

Palm-tree wood—Mr. B. Rich, Fernandina, Florida.

Stone tomahawk—Marietta, Pennsylvania.

Stone pipe—Sioux, Missouri River, Dakota.

Wooden beads—Chinaman, San Francisco.

Moss agates—Wyoming Territory.

Indian hair—Sioux, Ponca River, Dakota.

Cinnamon bear's claw—Wyoming Territory.

Fire relics—Chicago, Illinois, October, 1871.

Knife sheath—Sioux, Cheyenne River, Dakota.

Stone tomahawk—Grant Siple, Washington, Penn.

Flint spear-head—Juniata County, Pennsylvania.

Petrified shells—Lakes Erie and Michigan.

Knife sheath—Park's Fort, Kansas.

Gold, silver, lead, copper—Colorado and Nevada.

Flint arrow-heads—Florida, Prof. S. S. Haldeman.

Indian pottery—vicinity of Amelia River, Florida.

Buffalo horns and teeth—Plains of Kansas.

Red pipe-stone—Sioux Indian Quarry, Minnesota.

Sea-beans—Captain J. F. Rich, Fernandina, Fla.

Petrified shark-teeth—Charleston, South Carolina.

Petrified bone—Bluffs of Southern Dakota.
Petrified wood—Colorado and California.
Stone image—Mr. J. Hanes, Wrightsville, Penn.
Sea-shells, star-fish, etc.—Fernandina, Florida.
Indian drawings—Sioux, Ponca River, Dakota.

PHOTOGRAPHS.

Spotted Tail and Two Strike, Sioux chiefs.
Fast Dog, Sioux warrior.
Little Crow, Sioux chief, executed for leading the
    Minnesota massacre of 1862.
Scalp of Little Crow.
Crossing Sky, Bad Boy and Big Dog, chiefs of the
    Chippewa bands.
Jim, Pahute chief.
Washakie, Shoshonee chief.
Groups of various bands.
Scenes in Salt Lake City.
Brigham Young and Joseph Smith.

CHAPTER VI.

There is a time—'tis evening—
  When the swallows homeward fly ;
When the golden rays of sunset
  Gild anew the western sky ;
When the varied forms of life,
  Throughout Nature cease to roam,
But for me, the weary wanderer,
  There seems to be no home.

Thus I ever, ever wander,
  While the seasons come and go,
Ever searching—never finding,
  What my heart so longs to know ;
But the searching will be ended,
  And the wanderer cease to roam,
When, at last, he really finds
  His own dear ideal home.
                                    L. G. WILSON.

RED MAN, MOVE ON—YANKTON CITY—DAKOTA—THE SANTEE
INDIANS—BAKING BREAD IN THE BABY'S WASH-PAN—THE
PRAIRIE GRASS—MINNESOTA—DETROIT—NIAGARA FALLS—
BUFFALO—LANCASTER CITY AND COUNTY—PENNSYLVANIA—
MY RESTLESSNESS—BROOKLYN—NEW HAVEN—PROVIDENCE—
BOSTON—ALBANY—TROY—A RACE WITH A LOCOMOTIVE—
HOW A DISHONEST COUPLE, IN KANSAS, SECURED A FARM.

THE site of Yankton City, the capital of Dakota,
was once occupied by the camp of "Shah-pah Mah-
to," (Dirty Bear,) a chief of the Yankton Sioux. At
the time of my first visit to the place in 1872, it
was a small frontier town, sixty-five miles from the
nearest railroad. Passing through the place, on my

way to the Indian country, during the summers of
1873, 1874, 1877 and 1878, I found it to be a very
thriving, energetic city, teeming with life and business. It now contains numerous blocks of brick
business houses and other buildings, beside many
handsome and costly private residences. Yankton
has become a railroad town, and also communicates
with Upper Dakota and Montana by a line of fine
Missouri River steamboats.

Prior to the year 1858, what is now known as
Dakota, was unceded land, and belonged to the
Sioux Indians. In that year a treaty was made
with the Sioux, and the land taken from them; it
was not organized as a territory, however, until the
winter of 1861.

During the years 1862 and 1863, the immigration
to Dakota was almost entirely stopped by the Sioux
war. Hundreds of settlers were killed in Minnesota and Dakota at that time; but a great change
has since taken place, and the fine soil and lovely
prairies and valleys are rapidly luring emigrants to
seek homes within its borders.

Dakota is very large, and as yet, only a small
part of it, comparatively, is settled by the whites,
the remainder being still the hunting-ground of the
Sioux and other Indian tribes.

I spent a short time in a Santee Sioux camp in a
large grove of wild plum trees, near Yankton, and
met there an old time-worn warrior, who on the oc-

casion of an Indian raid, I was informed, took an infant out of its cradle and thrust it into the fire, thus roasting it alive.

This heartless old fiend, after some conversation in broken English and by means of signs, showed me a beautiful red stone pipe and tomahawk combined, for which he wanted some "mus-is-cow," or money. After purchasing it I left the village, concluding my first visit among the Sioux. The tomahawk is now in the collection of Prof. Haldeman.

The next day I went to the main camp of the Santees, situated about thirty miles further up the Missouri, on the Nebraska side. These Indians are the remnant of the band of Sioux that committed the terrible massacre of men, women and children, at New Ulm, Minnesota, in 1862, under the leadership of Little Crow.

The Indian women, in general, are not noted for cleanliness in their cooking arrangements, and not a few of their customs, in this branch. often remind me of a statement made by the wife of an Indian missionary, who said that when dining with an Indian family in New Mexico, she ate bread that was baked in the pan the baby had been washed in.

Leaving the Indians, I returned to Sioux City, and then started for St. Paul. At that time the railroad between St. Paul and Sioux City was not completed, and I walked from Le Mars to Iona, a point just reached by the railroad graders.

As I walked alone over the then almost unsettled prairies of Northwestern Iowa, I found the luxuriant grass, in some places, from seven to nine feet high. Its rankness and height were often a source of much annoyance to me, as it sometimes hid the surrounding country from view, so that I could not see whether I was traveling in the right direction or not.

Minnesota, from its southern boundary to Fort Ripley, a point about two hundred miles northward, is a most enchanting prairie country, pleasantly interspersed with lovely lakes, whose pebbled shores are fringed with romantic little groves. This is a fair representative of the natural features of the whole state, excepting the northern part, which consists of dense pine forests.

There are thousands of miniature lakes in Minnesota, all clear, glittering and abounding in fish. In the northern forests deer, bear and other game are quite plenty. Minnesota is a Sioux Indian word, and signifies "cloudy, or turbid water." It has always been the favorite hunting-ground of the Sioux.

After spending a few days in St. Paul, I went to Milwaukee, and thence to Chicago. Then, passing through Northern Indiana, I visited the flourishing city of Detroit, the metropolis of Michigan. It is situated on a neck of water that connects Lakes Erie and Huron. Large quantities of grain, pork and copper-ore are shipped to Eastern cities. The early history of Detroit was one of struggles and battles against the hostile Indians of the surrounding country.

Leaving Detroit, I started for Buffalo, passing on through Canada, to the Suspension Bridge and Niagara Falls. As the traveler stands on the grand old weather-beaten Table Rock and looks on the mighty sheet of bright blue water, or lingers on the narrow foot-path under the falls, the vastness, the power of the falls is only first recognized. Its dimensions, breadth and volume might be given, but that would not be doing justice to Niagara Falls. A pen description cannot convey a true or satisfactory conception of its power and majestic grandeur.

Buffalo is situated at the eastern extremity of Lake Erie, and is a great thoroughfare for travel and traffic between the East and the West. Regular lines of fine iron steamships ply between this port and Erie, Cleveland, Toledo, Detroit, Chicago, Milwaukee, Duluth and other lake towns. Beside these, there are many sailing-vessels and steamboats constantly arriving and departing, during the navigable season; the Great Lakes being fresh water, navigation closes for a short time during the winter.

On my way home, I passed through the staid old city of Lancaster, Pennsylvania. This place was founded in the early days of Pennsylvania's settlement, and has many of the characteristics of an old town. It is the county seat of Lancaster County,

which has been justly called, "The Garden of the
Keystone State."

My travels have taken me into every state in the
Union, except one, and without egotism or undue
laudation, I freely assert that for beautiful farms,
fine buildings, comfortable and happy homes, where
peace and plenty abide, bright streams, charming
valleys and delightful groves, Lancaster County,
Pennsylvania, is superior to any district of country
I ever visited.

Perhaps one of the most pleasing features of the
locality is its generous, friendly people.   The quiet,
unassuming farmers of Lancaster County are noted
for these traits, and their kind-hearted, sensible and
plainly-attired wives and daughters, are an excellent
model for some of their giddy, loose-tongued, shallow, gossiping town sisters.

No one, who has mingled much with the world,
could travel long among the farming community of
Pennsylvania without learning that the truer forms
of Christianity, and the finer sensibilities of the
human heart, are more generally found in rural districts, than it is amid the city's din and strife.

While in Pennsylvania, I made several local journeys through Lancaster, York, Dauphin, Cumberland, Perry and Lebanon Counties.   These are all
agricultural districts, and contain a large portion
of the wealth and population of the State, also the
most beautiful and productive valleys.

After visiting my home, I made a tour through the New England States, for I could not content myself, or remain long at one place, and this restless spirit ever kept me wandering from one point to another. Within late years, however, I have become weary of traveling, and now as earnstly desire to settle down, as I once did to travel.

I had become so accustomed to camping out in the West, and "roughing it" generally, that I could not sleep well in a bed, upon returning to civilization, but preferred to lie upon the floor or other hard surface. The rumbling of car-wheels and the noise of a puffing steamboat always made me restless and uncomfortable unless I was going along with them; and in dreams, I was often carried back to the land of my Indian friends and their wild, romantic surroundings.

On my way North I visited the various cities on my route, also those upon the course by which I returned. I always wanted to see everything in my reach, and I generally deemed time, trouble and fatigue a secondary consideration.

Brooklyn, separated from New York City by the East River, contains a population of nearly half a million people. Here reside many of the business men of New York. Steamboats run between the two cities every few minutes during the day.

New Haven is situated on a small bay, four miles from Long Island Sound. It is the seat of Yale

College, and is noted for its extensive manufactures.

Providence is the semi-state capital of Rhode Island, and is the second city, in size, in New England. It is located at the head of Narraganset Bay, and is connected with surrounding cities by a network of railroads.

Boston is one of the oldest and most interesting cities in the United States. Here were enacted some of the most eventful phases of the Colonial War. Beside being a great manufacturing city, it is especially noted for its many benevolent, art and literary institutions. Boston may well be called the home of authors, the work-shop of printers and the market-place of publishers. It is an important seaport, and does a large shipping trade with all parts of the world.

Upon leaving the state of Maine, on my return journey, I visited Concord, Manchester, Nashua and Fitchburg, and then on to Troy by way of the Hoosac Tunnel.

Troy is situated on the Hudson River, six miles above Albany and at the head of navigation. It is largely engaged in manufacturing stoves, steel, etc.

Albany, the capital of New York, is a beautiful, stirring and wealthy city. During the summer, fine steamboats run on the Hudson River, between Albany and New York City. The Hudson is famed for its beauty and the grandeur of the scenery on its banks.

From Albany I continued southward. Reaching Gun Powder River (which might be more properly called back-water from Chesapeake Bay), between Philadelphia and Baltimore, with a fellow-traveler, late one night, we proceeded to walk over the railroad bridge, which was merely a trestle-work about a mile in length. All we had to walk upon was a board about a foot wide, placed upon the cross-ties.

When about half way across the bridge we were startled by the shrill whistle of a locomotive, and, upon turning round, we saw to our horror, the headlight of the south-bound express just entering upon the trestle-work. I had faced death before, but as I saw the fiery, puffing engine approaching like some enraged demon ready to destroy me, I felt as though my time had now come.

There being but a single track upon the trestle, there was no room to hold on to any part of it until the train would pass. Only one avenue of escape was open to us, and that was flight. The frost of the night made the foot-board so slippery that we were liable, at every bound, to plunge into the freezing water beneath.

There was no time to lose, for the train was so near, that it shook the board we were upon. So, on and on we went, while the ponderous, roaring locomotive gained upon us at every revolution of its wheels. We knew that life depended upon our exertion, and we pressed onward without faltering.

A lifetime of thought was condensed into the time of a few moments. My comfortable home, kind mother and my early childhood days, vividly appeared to my mind. At last, faint and terrified, we reached the end of the bridge, just in time to leap aside and escape from being crushed by the locomotive at our heels.

The remainder of the night we walked along the railroad, and suffered severely from the inclemency of the weather, as every place where we might have secured shelter, was closed for the night. Early in the morning, however, we noticed a light a short distance ahead of us, and upon approaching nearer, we found that it proceeded from a small cabin. We soon reached the house, and were kindly entertained by the inmates, a genteel colored family.

From Baltimore I went to Cincinnati, and then returned to Philadelphia, where I clerked in a store until spring, when I started for Kansas.

When about to cross the Steubenville Bridge, on the Pan Handle Railway, on my way from Cincinnati to Philadelphia, the train I was on ran into another passenger-train just after it had crossed the bridge. For a few minutes after the shock, a panic raged among the passengers, but fortunately no person was injured, not even the engineer or fireman of either train, for after doing all in their power to check the speed of their trains, they jumped from their engines before they collided.

A frontier town is an object of interest. The streets, which are either muddy or dusty, in the spring of the year, are thronged with emigrants waiting for an opportunity to "enter their claims" upon the free land they have selected. Groups of cattle-herders, hunters and ranchmen, dressed in buckskin and carrying the indispensable revolver, are constantly to be seen, as well as small parties of Indians who come to town to do their trading.

An energetic, but dishonest married couple, in Kansas, took advantage of "Uncle Sam," to the extent of a farm, in this wise: They had secured a homestead in the customary way, but not satisfied with one farm, and desiring the unoccupied section adjoining their land, they secured a divorce by misrepresenting their family affairs, and when the late wife became an unmarried woman, she was entitled to 160 acres of Government land; so she obtained the free tract next to the farm of her late husband, after which they were married again.

CHAPTER VII.

See! a dusky line approaches: hark! the onward, surging roar,
Like the din of wintry breakers on a sounding wall of shore;
Dust and sand behind them whirling, snort the foremost of the van,
And their stubborn horns are clashing through the crowded caravan.

Myriad hoofs will scar the prairie, in our wild, resistless race,
And a sound, like mighty waters, thunders down the desert space:
Yet the rein may not be tightened, nor the rider's eyes look back—
Death to him whose speed should slacken, on the angry bison's track!

Look not on him as he staggers,—'tis the last shot he will need!
More shall fall, among his fellows, ere we run the mad stampede,—
Ere we stem the brinded breakers, while the wolves, a hungry pack,
Howl around each grim-eyed carcass, on the bloody bison's track!

BAYARD TAYLOR.

I JOIN A PARTY OF BUFFALO HUNTERS—A STORM—THE CAMP
FIRE—LIFE OF A HUNTER—WILLOW SPRINGS—THE FIRST
BUFFALO—A PRAIRIE FIRE—A SCENE OF CONFUSION—THE
POWDER—AN ANCIENT LAND MARK—BUFFALO TRAILS—THE
BEAUTY OF SUNSET ON THE PRAIRIES—THE WILD HORSE OF
THE PLAINS—O'FALLON'S CAMP—HUNTING THE BISON.

AFTER a short stay at Topeka and Ellsworth, I
moved on to Fort Wallace. Here I joined a party
of buffalo hunters, who were about to start for the
Republican River, about ninety miles north of the
fort. Our outfit consisted of three hunters and myself, four horses and two wagons for hauling hides,
a set of cooking utensils, several Sharps' rifles, a
supply of provisions, blankets and ammunition.

The first day we did not travel far, owing to a

storm which prevailed. The wind blew a perfect hurricane, and filled the air with sand and gravel, even pebbles were blown about with such force as greatly to annoy the horses, as well as ourselves. Finally, we concluded to camp in a deep ravine till morning, hoping the storm would then abate.

After unhitching the horses and securing them to a stake, by means of a lariat, some "buffalo-chips" were gathered, with which a fire was made. Supper was next prepared, the meal consisting of warm bread, baked in a Dutch oven, meat and coffee.

I used the skull of a dead buffalo as a stool at the supper-table, which consisted of the original prairie-sod, while the hunters seated themselves on the ground, Indian-fashion. When the meal was over, we spent several hours in conversation.

My companions were brave, true-hearted men, and had spent years on the plains, hunting, trapping and scouting. I became warmly attached to them, and will ever remember them kindly. If I ever meet them again, or learn their whereabouts, it will afford me great pleasure to present each one of them a copy of my narrative, in memory of the pleasant weeks I passed with them on the western plains of Kansas. Unfortunately, however, I have no clue to their present abiding place, neither do I know their proper names, for they were known on the plains as, Pat, Short-cake Henry, Legs, English, Mc Cabe and Tarantula Jack.

When bedtime arrived some blankets and robes
were laid upon the ground, under one of the wagons, and a large piece of canvas was then spread
over the wagon and fastened to the wheels; thus
making a very snug tent, where we slept warm and
comfortable.

The next morning after breakfast, we proceeded
on our way, but the wind was still so strong that
we traveled but a few miles, and then camped again
in a ravine.   There was no water near, and as we
did not want to dispense with "our coffee," some
snow, that had fallen during the night, was gathered and melted, the grass and sand which adhered
to it, not injuring the flavor of the coffee.

The following day we reached a small valley, or.
rather a meadow, containing several pools of standing, alkaline water, which are known to hunters and
bordermen generally, as Willow Springs.   They are
situated about fifteen miles north of Fort Wallace.

A few hundred yards from the springs, one of the
hunters shot a huge male buffalo that was alone on
the bluff-side browsing.   So here we concluded to
camp until the weather became calm.

One of our men, not using proper caution while
starting a fire for cooking purposes, came very near
causing the death of the whole party.   The grass
around us being rank and dry, it ignited immediately, and fanned by the strong wind, the flames
almost surrounded us before we could comprehend

our situation. The horses had not been unhitched, and springing into the wagons, the terrified beasts bore us rapidly away.

On, and on we went, the fire gaining upon us all the time, while the prairie and meadow behind us, now appeared like a great, rolling wave of hissing, rushing, roaring flame. Shortly the fire curled up around the wagons, and in a few minutes more, the horses were bounding through the fire.

At this juncture, one of the hunters exclaimed: "Look out for the powder!" and the fright and confusion that followed, can not well be described. The powder was carried for reloading the metallic cartridge-shells for the breech-loading rifles, and there was a quantity of it in the wagons.

One of the men, having more presence of mind than the rest of us, turned the horses, with some difficulty, and drove them back on to the burned district, where we were comparatively safe. Not having taken any of the utensils out of the wagons, nothing was destroyed by the fire. But the horses were severely scorched, and we were all well singed upon the hands and face.

As the fire started some distance from where the buffalo was shot, and as the wind was coming in the right direction to carry the flames still further away, the animal was not scorched in the least.

After pulling up some grass, and burning a space around us, in order to have a bare place, and consequently a safe one, to camp on, the buffalo was skinned and the choice parts of the meat secured.

All night long the fire raged around us, and for miles the plains appeared like a mighty sea of fiery billows, that illuminated the earth and sky with a fearful, yet majestic glare. Watch was kept during the night, lest after all our precautions, the wind changing, would drive the fire upon us from some other direction. For a day after, the air was black and stifling, and our course was strewn with the bones of animals that had fallen a prey to the fire.

Wood was very scarce all along the way, and frequently, we did not see a particle in a day's travel. But "buffalo-chips" could be found in great abundance, and they were an excellent substitute, for a hotter and more lasting fire could be made with them than could be produced with wood.

I can remember of seeing but one fair-sized tree, or part of one rather, between Fort Wallace and the Republican. Just before reaching the Willow Springs, we came to the trunk of a large tree destitute of bark and branches, and standing alone on the prairie.

The buffaloes had resorted to this old land-mark for years, as a means of relief from fleas, and it was worn as smooth as glass where the monsters had rubbed their shaggy sides against it. There were numerous buffalo-trails leading from the streams, many miles distand, to this old trunk. The trails had been worn to a depth of ten and twelve feet.

During the next few days we traveled over a section of the American Desert, after which we came to a very beautiful prairie country, abounding with buffaloes, antelope, wolves and prairie-dogs.

No more buffaloes were killed than were deemed necessary for present use, as the hunters were on their way to the Republican River in order to get some hides which they had left there to dry, when on the previous hunt.

The country on all sides of us, swarmed with the bison. So great were their numbers, that at times, the plains, for miles in extent, were covered with immense herds of the animals; and the dust caused by the thousands of restless hoofs, arose around them like a cloud. At times we were obliged to halt and let them pass us, for in their wild, unwavering gallops they were liable to crush us beneath their ponderous hoofs.

It was now about the middle of April, and the storm being over, the sun made its appearance, to the great delight of our little party. The grass soon began to sprout, the first delicate blossoms of spring pushed forth, the birds fluttered about with loud and joyous melodies and all Nature seemed to rejoice at the change.

To the lover of Nature, a feeling of mingled sadness and pleasure is experienced by the effect of a sunset on the prairies. The golden beams stream

along the surface of the ever waving grass and tinge
it with a gorgeous hue, as the great orb of declining day buries itself in the distant ocean of boundless ether.   Then slowly the face-like moon seems
to emerge from the eastern horizon, and proceeds
along the starry sky.

Soon the solemnity of night prevails.   The notes
of warbling birds are no longer heard, and the buffaloes and antelope are at rest.   There is no moving
to and fro of the hunter, or stampeding of the startled herd.   Occasionally, the sharp, piercing yelp of
the gray wolf and coyote sounds upon the still air,
but all else is silent; Nature, like the weary traveler,
has ended the duties of the day, and He who never
sleeps watches over all.

One day we discovered three wild horses grazing
in a beautiful little meadow, about half a mile distant. We endeavored to get near them unobserved,
but they scented us, and then, with a toss of their
beautiful heads, bounded swiftly away, and shortly
after disappeared behind a ridge of grassy bluffs.

They were perfect beauties, jet black and glossy,
with mane and tail almost touching the ground.   It
was a grand sight to see them galloping over the
green prairies and slopes at a speed that bid defi-
ance to all pursuers.

One night we camped in a very large and deep
cavity, which had the appearance of having been
formed by volcanic eruption at some remote period

of time. The place is known to hunters and trappers as "O'Fallon's Camp," and as it is close to the old "Starvation Trail," it very likely received that name from some adventurous guide, while escorting a company of emigrants across the plains, in the early days of immigration to California.

While approaching the place, we were almost surrounded by an immense herd of buffaloes, which, owing to its size, and a number of little calves that were with it, made very slow progress, and we were obliged to stop and let it pass.

The time for camping, in the evening, was hailed with delight, for then we could rest from the march and have a good time around the camp-fire. Warm as the day may be, on the plains, the night air is cool and bracing.

Our camp was always pitched in the same general position, on the approach of evening, and the duty of frying meat, making coffee and baking bread was about the same at each camp.

In some places, along our route, the ground was strewn with the carcasses of bison that had been slain merely for their hides. I have seen the plains, for miles on every hand, so thickly strewn with dead buffaloes that it was difficult to travel with a team. Sometimes the hunters will decoy and follow up a large herd for days, finally slaying the last animal.

When they desire to shoot a number of buffaloes, they first kill a few of the females, when the rest

of the herd generally crowd around the fallen ones,
bellowing and moaning in a manner painful to hear.
The hunters then lie concealed in the grass, and
shoot them down at leasure. In this way, one man
often kills fifty buffaloes before he rises from his
place of ambush.

So long as the game does not see the foe, or scent
him, it will linger about the dead and wounded companions. For meat, young cows are singled out of
a herd, and after securing the tongue, a part of one
of the hind-quarters, and perhaps a piece of liver,
the rest is left for the wolves and vultures.

No little danger is incurred while hunting. At
times, a herd will suddenly become frightened, and
dashing away in a moment, will crush both hunters
and horses beneath their feet. In a close encount-
er, the hunter, after seeing his game fall, retires to
a safe distance, in order to avoid the terrible death
lunge which a badly wounded bison seldom fails to
make, for, although the animal may fall at the first
shot, it generally regains its feet before dropping
in death.

Although I have seen many thousands of bison,
and wasted no small amount of lead and patience
upon them, I never saw one drop under my aim. I
could kill a squirrel or a rabbit, and even a duck on
the wave, with a rifle or revolver, but I could not
bring down a buffalo at a distance of one hundred
yards, as I could not strike them in the heart.

CHAPTER VIII.

In the far-away land, where the buffaloes roam,
  Where balmy winds fan the plains of the west;
'Mid lovely flowers, of many hues,
  They laid the Indian maiden to rest.

Where merry birds, with brightest wings,
  Sing their songs above her grave,
And the moonbeam's calm and pearly rays,
  With weeping-willows, o'er it wave.

A. H. G.

THE REPUBLICAN RIVER AND VALLEY—AN INDIAN MAIDEN'S GRAVE AMONG THE BRANCHES OF A WEEPING WILLOW—MEDITATIONS—SNOW WATER AS A LUXURY—THE SINGULAR EFFECTS OF MIRAGE ON THE PLAINS—PANGS OF HUNGER—EATING RAW MEAT—THE SMOKY HILL RIVER.

ABOUT noon of the last day's travel, our eager eyes beheld the high bluffs on the north bank of the Republican River, and upon going a little further, the course of the river could be traced by the belt of timber and shrubbery that grew upon its banks.

Soon we could see the water sparkling in the sun, and appearing in the distance, like a mere thread of silver, when a shout of joy and thankfulness arose from our thirsty, jaded little company.

At the river we found three other hunters who had been left to take care of the hides which we were in quest of. The names of the new members were Tarantula Jack, Legs and English. They had

built themselves a rude hut on a hill-side, both for
a dwelling place, and as a means of protection from
the Indians.

The Republican at this point is both narrow and
shallow, although it amply waters a lovely little
valley, the green grass, budding flowers, trees and
vines of which, formed a pleasing contrast to some
of the dry, dusty plains we had traversed.

In the bosom of this beautiful, secluded valley,
where the river formed a semi-circle, inclosing a
charming, grass-covered plat of ground, stood a
solitary weeping-willow tree, in whose branches had
been placed the dead body of a young Sioux Indian
woman, in accordance with one of their modes of
disposing of the dead.

The tree stood within a few feet of the river's
edge, and the drooping branches almost touched
the bright, rippling water.

My companions were some distance away, and as
I stood there alone, with nothing to mar my meditations and the solemn calm that prevailed, save the
low, pleasant murmur of the peaceful river as it
flowed on its lonely course, I was strangely impressed with the idea of death in this enchanting oasis,
far from the din, contention and vexation of the
world, and of a grave among the green boughs of
a drooping-willow, with the bright sunshine, sparkling water and singing birds for companions.

The eagles and vultures had visited the body

sometime before, and scattering the bones on the ground beneath the tree, left them for the wolves to pick, and the sun to bleach. At the foot of the tree, among the bones, I found a small buckskin bag containing some sugar, also a bunch of black thread. The Indians had deposited these articles with the body.

As I turned to leave the spot, with sadness and awe, it occurred to my mind that the finely bleached and symmetrically formed skull would be far better preserved among my Indian mementos, than in the Valley of the Republican, where it would be crushed by the ponderous hoofs of the buffaloes; but I left it where I found it, believing that if its late immortal tenant could express its wish, it would be to leave it to crumble to dust on the moss-grown bank of the peaceful river.

The bluffs in the vicinity of the river, were almost constantly thronged with buffaloes going to and from the water, and the hunters would lie in the grass and shoot them at pleasure.

After resting a few days, the buffalo-hides were placed upon the wagons, when we started to return to Fort Wallace. Leaving the Republican behind us with regret, we started to cross the monotonous expanse of prairies, sand-hills, bluffs and ravines that lay in our course.

The weather, during the day, was now warm and sultry, and when we arrived at O'Fallon's Camp, I

filled the water-kegs with snow, which I found in
the deep gorges that were protected from the sun
by over-hanging rocks and shrubbery; and while
it lasted, we had a luxury rare and refreshing.

The mirage on the Western Prairies is a singular
phænomenon, which might be termed Nature's art
of photography. This illusion is caused by the re-
flection of the sun's rays upon objects remote from
the place where the mirage portrays them.

Towns, mountains, forests, lakes and rivers are
often seen in the veil-like, waving halo that limits
the scope of sight, and appears like the white glow
of intense heat rising from the earth.

No matter how long the traveler may journey in
the direction of the objects pictured, he will never
reach them, and they will appear no nearer than
when he first noticed them. Many men have died
from the indescribable agony of thirst, while hunting the sheet of pure, transparent water that the
false, fascinating mirage had represented to them.

On account of the intense transparency of the
atmosphere on the plains, objects can be seen at an
almost incredible distance. A band of Indians, or
a herd of buffalo can be distinguished, on a clear
day, at a distance of twenty and thirty miles. A
ridge of bluffs that may appear to be no more than
ten miles distant, is frequently three times as far.
At Willow Springs, thirteen miles from the Kansas
Pacific Railroad, I plainly saw the cars running on

the track, and could readily distinguish the engine
from the other cars, as well as see the smoke rising
from the stack.

The ever snow-capped Pike's Peak, in Colorado,
can be seen from the Kansas Pacific Railroad, at a
point eighty miles distant, towering grandly among
the fleecy clouds, from which at first sight, it is difficult to recognize it. It can also be seen from the
Platte River, at a distance of over a hundred miles.

When about sixty miles from Fort Wallace, we
found ourselves short of provisions, owing to negli-
gence on the part of the hunter whose duty it was
to lay in the supplies, and as we were in a section
of country where game was very scarce, the pangs
of hunger soon commenced to be keenly felt.

Troubles, it is said, never come singly, and this
was our experience. In addition to the low state of
our stores, and the scarcity of game, we lost the
trail, and after traveling for miles in various directions, at random, the horse-feed became exhausted,
just as we were about entering upon a sandy desert
destitute of grass. As a natural consequence of the
new misfortune, the over-burdened horses became
weak, and therefore, could travel but slowly.

When the flour was all used, and the last piece
of bread was dealt out, our prospects were gloomy.
One of the men divided the only remaining bread
into seven equal parts. This was to be shared out
among the six famishing persons, and after each of

us had received a share—a piece about two inches square—the seventh part remained. With one accord, my companions declared that, "the stranger must have it," and with all cheerfulness, the mite of bread was given to me.

The hunters held out well, and seemed to find relief from the gnawings of hunger, by a free use of tobacco, but never having used the weed, save for friendship's sake when among the Indians, I could not resort to such means successfully.

For three days and nights we fasted, with the exception, however, that the hunters had the tobacco and I retained a handful of green coffee. The last piece of buffalo meat we had on the trip, we pretended to roast on the fire, but the most of it was eaten raw, for we were too hungry to be particular about the cooking.

The hunters became so weak and nerveless from want of food, that when an occasional group of antelope or buffaloes made its appearance, they were unable to shoot accurately enough to kill any.

One night, toward the end of the journey, two of the horses wandered away, and thus put a stop to our traveling for a time. Finally, we concluded to push on to Willow Springs with one team, where I remained with it, while the hunters started out in different directions in search of the lost horses.

I remained alone all day, and taking one of the rifles and some cartridges, I searched the prairies and bluffs for a buffalo or an antelope, but in vain.

In the evening the hunters returned with the missing horses, and the next day we reached the little town of Wallace, on the Kansas Pacific Railroad, three miles from Fort Wallace.

Soon after arriving, we proceeded to the Railroad House, where we did justice to the ample meal that had been prepared for us.

During our long and painful fast of three days and nights, my companions bore up well, and were even cheerful and in good spirits; but with me it was otherwise. After giving me the last mouthful of bread, they doubtless, through kindness for me, endeavored to cheer and encourage me, by hiding all evidences of their own suffering.

Toward the end of the journey, the gnawings of hunger were keenly felt by me, and the singular optical illusion of an abundance of food and the actual ceremony of feasting at a table filled with luxuries, were most vividly presented to my eyes and mind by an influence that I am unable to account for.

I could see my mother at home frying meat, and I imagined that I saw the fat bubbling up in the pan, and smelled the tempting odor of the meat. I had always been very fond of apple-dumplings, and (according to my way of seeing things at that time) huge piles of them were lying upon the desert.

One day, while in New York City, I noticed in

one of the markets, a German woman selling batter-
cakes, and now, in my singular condition of mind, I
fancied myself eating batter-cakes without number.
I distinctly remember of making a vow to myself,
that if I ever reached civilization again, I would
have a woman to bake cakes for me from morning
till night.

The cause of these singular freaks of the mind,
was probably due to the pangs of hunger and the
weakness of the general system, brought on by the
want of food.

Before going further west, I visited the Smoky
Hill River. This stream received its name from
the presence of a veil of dim and dreamy vapor,
which during the summer, continually hangs over
the river and surrounding mounds.

The vicinity of this river, at certain times of the
year, is a favorite hunting-ground of the Cheyenne,
Pawnee and Sioux Indians, it being an excellent
buffalo range. Here the Indians also catch many
wild horses by means of the lasso.

I visited the river alone, and all Nature seemed
wrapped in a serene repose that was most delightful to one who loves the sweet calm of Nature's
solitude. The birds sang merrily over my head, the
peaceful river glided noiselessly along and the wind
was soft and balmy, but at times, assumed a deeper
tone, and rustled through the foliage in strains as
mournful as those of an Æolian harp.

CHAPTER IX.

I hear the tread of pioneers
    Of nations yet to be;
The first low wash of waves where soon
    Shall roll a human sea.

I hear the far-off voyager's horn;
    I see the Yankee's trail—
His foot on every mountain-pass,
    On every stream his sail.

Behind the scared squaw's birch canoe,
    The steamer smokes and raves,
And city lots are staked for sale
    Above old Indian graves.

WHITTIER.

MOUNTAIN SCENERY IN COLORADO—THE CACTUS PLANT ON ITS NATIVE SOIL—A LONELY JOURNEY THROUGH THE WILDS—"ROUGHING IT"—HOW THE BUFFALOES DIMINISH—THE UTE INDIAN—MODE OF SACRIFICING INDIAN PONIES—EMIGRANTS IN CAMP—LOST ON THE PRAIRIES AT NIGHT—CHICAGO—A SCHOOL FOR THE STUDY OF HUMAN NATURE—THE MISSOURI RIVER COUNTRY—A BEAUTIFUL LAND—I VISIT THE SIOUX—A FRIENDLY SQUAW—RUDENESS OF THE ARICKAREES.

FROM Fort Wallace I went to Denver, and then down to Colorado Springs and the Garden of the Gods, at the foot of Pike's Peak; finally reaching Pueblo by way of the Denver & Rio Grande Railroad, and the old Santa Fe wagon-trail, which runs along the base of the Rocky Mountains.

The mountain scenery in Colorado is very grand.

Beautiful streams of clear, sparkling water, fed by the ever snow-capped peaks, dizzy heights, fearful precipices and mighty cataracts, meet the eye on every side.

Along the foot of the mountains, in this section, is to be found a species of the tall, branching cactus, covering vast tracts of land. I found many of the stalks from four to eight feet in height. This plant, like the sage-brush and prickly-pear, is gen erally found in sandy, barren places, and does not thrive well if removed to a more fertile locality.

I procured some of the cactus seed, and sent it on to Mr. Joseph Windolph, a florist of Marietta, Pennsylvania. This gentleman succeeded in raising a healthy stalk, but upon being transplanted, it drooped and died, the soil not being suitable for it.

From the old Mexican town of Pueblo I started for Sargent, Kansas, which was then the terminus of the Atchison, Topeka & Santa Fe Railroad, one hundred and fifty miles distant. My route was along the banks of the Arkansas River, and I made the journey alone, armed only with a revolver.

At times, I subsisted upon rabbits which I shot along the way and roasted upon forked sticks; and occasionally I found a lone ranchman, when I was always kindly received and hospitably entertained.

One day, after having walked about a week, I reached a solitary log hut, and, to my great aston ishment, I saw through the open door, a white

woman making bread, and a baby quietly sleeping
in its cradle. Such a domestic scene I never expected to see in a country which was still the home
of the Indians and buffaloes.

Her husband was hunting game, or performing
some other pioneer duty, but the good wife warmly
welcomed me, and was as much pleased and surprised to see a white face as I was. She did not
appear to fear the Indians, and judging by a huge
revolver that was lying in the room, I supposed
she would have shown battle, had they attempted
to molest her or her household.

For miles along the river, between Bent's Fort
and Fort Lyon, the ground was strewn with thousands of dead buffaloes that had been killed during
the previous winter merely for their hides, which
at Fort Dodge, were worth two dollars apiece.

At the time of my journey, the spring of 1873,
the Arkansas Valley was an unsettled district, and
the roaming ground of the Cheyenne, Arapahoe
and Ute Indians; but a marvelous change has been
wrought since that time. The red men have gone
further into the interior, the locomotive now thunders through the country from the Missouri to the
Rio Grande, and the grazing-ground of the bison
has been turned into wheat fields.

One day I met a Mexican riding upon a mustang
pony, and coming up to me, he addressed me in
Mexican and asked me for some tobacco. Unable

to accommodate him, and disliking his countenance,
I bade him adieu and started to leave him.   But he
detained me, and then tried to take my over-coat.
which I carried on my arm.

Becoming indignant at this, I looked straight into his glittering, snake-like eyes, and gave him to
understand that one Mexican could not well take
my coat.   He then rode away, and I resumed my
journey unmolested.

One evening I noticed some object on the roof
of a log hut, near the river.   Approaching it, I saw
that it was an Indian sleeping.   The house had
been deserted sometime before, and the Indian was
a member of a large band of Utes who had crossed
the river shortly before my arrival.

I climbed upon the roof, and after a short conversation, by means of signs, I shook hands with
him and then proceeded on my way.

In a little while, I came to the deserted camp of
the Indians.   The fires were still smoking, showing that the Utes had left but a short time before.
They had tortured a pony before leaving camp, and
I found it still alive and suffering terribly.

The flesh had been cut away from the lower jaw,
so that the bone was exposed.   Three wooden pins,
about a foot in length, had been forced through
the neck, and held in position by a piece of raw-
hide rope firmly tied around the throat.   When I
neared the pony, it strove violently, and groaned

with agony. I could have shot the poor creature, and relieved it from misery, but I feared the report of my revolver would bring a party of Indians upon me.

As I turned to leave, the animal moved its head and moaned piteously, as though asking me to help it. So I cut the thong and loosened the pins, this being all I could do in safety, and then proceeded on my lonely way.

At Sand Creek, near Fort Lyon, I passed the spot where Mrs. Clara Blynn and her little baby boy were captured by the Cheyenne Indians, in 1868, after the savages had killed most of the men belonging to the company of emigrants, of which Mrs. Blynn and child were members.

The captives were taken by Santama's party, and carried to a Kiowa Indian village on the Washita River. After suffering terribly at the hands of the savages, the mother and babe were killed by their cruel captors just as the late General Custer and his men charged upon the Indian camp.

While in Ottawa, Kansas, in the spring of 1878, I met Mrs. Blynn's parents, Mr. and Mrs. W. F. Harrington, and a sad and heart-rending account of the affair was given me by the aged and heartbroken parents. After the Indians fled from their village, the soldiers found Mrs. Blynn and her boy lying dead among the bodies of some of the fallen savages. Although the soldiers had a battle with

the Indians while Mrs. Blynn was in the camp, it
was not supposed that she was accidentally shot by
the troops, but was killed by the Indians because
they could not bear her away in the flight.

Major Elliott and his companions found the two
bodies lying close together, and after some prepar-
ation, tenderly carried them to one of the garrisons,
where, in one grave, the young mother and child
peacefully sleep.

While on this march I came to a camp of returning Arkansas emigrants, who had stopped for a few
days' rest. They greeted me with genuine border
hospitality, and as I was travel-worn and weary, I
concluded to stop with them a day or two and rest.

In the party was a boy about sixteen years old, a
bright, handsome young fellow, a good hunter and
one of the best marksmen I ever saw. We soon
became warm friends, and together, we had some
fine hunts. The river and prairie sloughs, in the
vicinity, were alive with wild geese and ducks, and
we could lie in the grass and shoot them at will.

I started for the settlement, about ten miles distant, one evening, thinking I would have no trouble
in finding the way. I was greatly mistaken in that,
however, and on the approach of darkness, I wandered among the disagreeable alkaline sloughs and
became utterly confused, not knowing which way to
turn, or in what direction the settlement was.

The sky was cloudy and threatening, and soon

the darkness of night came upon me. At times, I could not see ten steps ahead of me, save when the passing clouds momentarily permitted the rays of the moon to illuminate my dismal surroundings.

Sometimes, while groping through the tall and tangled grass, I would stumble into a pond with a loud splash, and the mingled cackling, shrieking and flapping of wings of the hundreds of ducks and geese that were frightened, broke upon the silent night air with a horrid and gloomy sound.

Hoping to attract the attention of the emigrants I had left, I discharged my revolver several times, but no answering salute was given, the emigrants probably fearing an Indian ambuscade. At every discharge of my pistol (my true and only companion on many a journey in the western wilds) flocks of ducks and geese arose from their resting place in great fright and confusion.

At last, after wandering about till after midnight, I espied, in the distance, the faint glow of a dying camp fire. I proceeded toward it immediately, and upon reaching it, I found myself at the camp of the emigrants I had left a few hours before.

After building up the fire, I dried my clothes, which had become drenched with water, and then, after taking a cup of hot coffee, I retired to one of the wagons, in which I slept soundly till morning.

The next day I reached Sargent, and after a short stay there, I proceeded on to Chicago, by way of

Emporia, Topeka, Atchison, Quincy and Galesburg.

Chicago, situated on the southwestern shore of Lake Michigan, is one of the most extraordinary evidences of American growth and development in the country. Chicago is said to be a Pottawatomie Indian word, meaning "the place of a skunk."

The site of the present city was mentioned by a Frenchman named Perrot, who visited the spot, a low marsh at the time, in 1671. The Government erected Fort Dearborn there in 1803, but it was destroyed by the Indians in 1812. In the year 1832 Chicago contained but a few families, now it is a great and growing city, containing half a million souls. In commercial importance, it ranks as the third or fourth city in the Union, but for business energy, rapid growth and all that is known by the term "fast," Chicago probably outstrips all other cities in the country.

Chicago is the largest wheat and live-stock mart in the world, as well as the greatest railroad center. It is estimated that about four hundred trains of cars enter and leave the city daily.

There is probably no better place for reading the human face—that printed index of the heart and mind—than on the crowded, bustling streets of a great city. Here the various forms of character and disposition are most strikingly portrayed; the kind and the unkind, the proud and the humble, the merry and the sad, the charitable and the un-

charitable, are all mingled together in one moving,
striving mass, traveling, apparently, unconsciously
and thoughtlessly, toward one goal—the grave!

After remaining several weeks in Chicago, I went
to Des Moines, and thence to Yankton, Dakota, at
which place I embarked in the steamboat *Miner* for
Fort Lincoln and Bismarck, about eight hundred
miles distant, by the course of the ever winding
Missouri River, though by land, the distance is not
much more than half as far.

We were two weeks in making the voyage, and
being the month of July, the mosquitoes were very
annoying. The officers and soldiers at the military
stations along the way, wore buckskin gloves, and
upon their hats and caps they had small hoops, to
which were fastened a piece of thin gauze, covering
the face and neck, thus securing protection against
the insects.

The boat was in charge of Captain Kelley and
Mr. Tim Burleigh, old Pennsylvanians and competent steamboat men.

The Missouri River, in many respects, is one of
the greatest and most interesting streams in the
world. It is the main feeder of the Mississippi,
after flowing in a very circuitous course for a distance of over three thousand miles, and draining
all of the country between the eastern base of the
Rocky Mountains and the Mississippi River divide.

The Missouri rises in the mountains of northwest

Montana, and its principal tributaries are the Yellow Stone, Little Missouri, Cheyenne, White Earth, Niobrara, Platte and Kansas Rivers. These secondary streams obtain their volume from the Tongue, Big Horn, Powder, Ponca, Loup Fork, Smoky Hill and Republican Rivers, and they, in turn, are fed by hundreds of creeks and rivulets.

All this vast ramification of water has been most judiciously distributed over the land of the mighty West by a kind Providence, and at once proclaims the lovely, blooming prairies to be a suitable home for many of the inhabitants of the crowded East.

Along the Missouri, in Dakota and Nebraska, are fine forests of cotton-wood, box-elder and willow. Shortly after leaving the river, however, the open prairie is reached, where no timber is found, except along the creeks and ravines. In some places, the treeless prairies and bluffs reach the river's brink, forming grand and picturesque lawns and uplands, all covered, during the summer months, with wild flowers and blossoms of the most beautiful hues.

The time can not be very far distant, when the settler's substantial cabin, his fields of wheat, herds of cattle and flocks of sheep, will be seen on this vast expanse of sea-like monotony. Surely, if there are anywhere, inviting farms and homes for many of the poor and oppressed of the densely crowded communities, they are to be found on the luxuriant prairies of the Far West.

Cannon Ball River, a tributary of the Missouri, is very pure and clear, and retains its own transparency for some distance after joining the muddy and turbulent receptacle. It received its name from the singular fact that its shores are lined with almost perfectly round stones resembling cannon balls.

On the Missouri, between Yankton and Bismarck, are situated Forts Randall, Sully, Pierre, Rice and Lincoln. The Indian agencies and trading posts, between the two points, are known as the Santee, Yankton, Crow Creek, Brule, Cheyenne, Grand and Standing Rock.

Most of the forts and agency buildings are constructed of native chalk-stone, and standing upon the bluffs overlooking the surrounding country for miles, they present a very imposing appearance.

The officers of the boat were very kind and accommodating to me; I remember Mr. A. Chapman, one of the crew, with respect, for many courtesies and attentions shown me.

Sometimes, when landing for wood, or to leave freight for the Government posts, I would go on shore to visit the Indians and see the country, accompanied by Mr. Chapman, who was thoroughly acquainted with the country and its wild, nomadic inhabitants.

As we steamed up the river, between its narrow fringes of cotton-wood and willow, we could see Indian life in most all of its various phases, and a

strange and vivid contrast was presented between
the savage life on shore, and the steam conveyance
of civilization ploughing its way through the water,
and carrying its evidences of the white man's en-
lightenment and power.

On the bluffs, just back of the river, as well as
in the timber along the banks, could be seen Indian
scaffolds, and hundreds of them were scattered all
along the way. The corpses had been placed upon these scaffoldings according to the customary
Sioux mode, and the red, blue and gray blankets
in which the bodies had been wrapped, could be
readily distinguished.

I was eager to go ashore sometimes, and examine
some of the deposits, but the officers of the boat
would not allow me to do so, as they feared the ire
of the Indians. The Sioux sometimes fire upon the
passing boats, and great care is therefore taken by
the officers to give them as little cause for hostility
as possible.

We frequently passed Indian villages scattered
for miles along the river, and hundreds of the inhabitants would watch us for hours, as we glided
around the bends of the ever-winding stream. At
times, they would follow us along the shore for a
distance of five and ten miles, demanding pay for
wood which we had obtained on the shore, for the
wood-yards were few and far apart.

One day I noticed several Sioux boys crawling

along the river bank with bows and arrows in their hands, and upon observing them closer, I saw that they were watching three ducks on the river. As our boat would have frightened the game before the Indians could get a fair shot at it, I raised my trusty revolver and fired. Two of the ducks arose and flew away, but the third was fished out of the water by the gratified Indians, and with many uncouth evidences of thanks to the white man, they climbed to the top of the steep bank, where they had a dance.

The boat stopped nearly a day at the Cheyenne River Indian Agency, and in the mean time, I went to a large village of Ogallala, Unkpapa and Minneconjon Sioux, situated about three miles from the agency. As I neared the camp, I noticed a number of Indians running about in great excitement, and I became much alarmed, for I did not know but that they were preparing to receive the lone visitor with murderous intent. But, as I learned shortly after, they were preparing to pursue a herd of runaway ponies.

At first, I was handled rather roughly by some of the young men, who gave me to understand that I was on dangerous ground, and that their stone war-clubs were just the thing to use in putting me out of the way.

I managed to get away from them, however, by seeking safety in a lodge occupied by an old squaw, and a girl about seventeen years of age—mother and daughter I supposed. Some of the Indians were about to follow me into the lodge, when the old squaw, to use an expression often heard among her white sisters, "gave them a piece of her mind," after which they left and troubled me no further.

The young squaw was the finest type of Indian beauty I ever saw; but I trust my lady readers will not doubt my assertion when I state that I am not near so much an admirer of female beauty, as I am of female kindness of heart, mildness of voice and manner, depth of mind, modesty of dress and deportment and a total absence of that loud, loose, giddy, gossiping tongue, that will ever repulse and disgust, no matter what the attractions of face or form may be.

The young squaw was seated on a robe when I entered, ornamenting a pair of handsome leggins, and upon looking up from her work, she greeted me very courteously, and bade me to be seated on a robe, while the old squaw, according to Indian politeness when entertaining visitors, placed some dried meat before me.

Before I left they presented me an ornamented knife-sheath and a string of beads, as mementos of my visit, and I, likewise, left them some trinkets.

In an Arickaree Indian camp, near Fort Lincoln, I was handled roughly, and some of the Indians assailed me with fire-brands.

Previous to my visit to the Sioux Indians near Cheyenne River Agency, I had very little experience with that tribe, knew but a few words of the language and was a stranger among them. But I have since made various journeys among the Sioux of Dakota, and have learned to speak with them in their own tongue, noted their customs and mode of life and have made warm friends among them.

The kindness, protection and hospitality that I received at their hands, when alone with them in their camps, far from the power of my own people, and surrounded by some of the most hostile Sioux in the West, will ever be the basis of kindly feeling and sympathy for this poor, down-trodden race.

In 1878, after returning from a two weeks' visit to Spotted Tail's main camp, then on Ponca River, Dakota, where I had been sent by a western journal, the *New York Herald* desired me to make an expedition to Sitting Bull's tribe for the purpose of furnishing letters for the paper, as well as to try to bring about a treaty of peace between Sitting Bull and the Government; but Secretary Schurz, upon being consulted by the *Herald* people, declined to favor the project. He probably had more faith in the efforts of the military in annihilating the tribe y attempting a second "Custer charge," than he ad in the efforts of a solitary man who was not a tranger among the Sioux, and who knew how to ain a point with them.

CHAPTER X.

To the west of Minnesota,
    And beyond the silv'ry Sioux,
Lies a country called Dakota
    Where the skies are ever blue;
So, stranger, come and find a home,
    If fortune you pursue,
'Tis a glorious land of prairies grand,
    And the skies forever blue.

                                JOHN BRENNAN.

SCENES IN BISMARCK—NORTH DAKOTA—I AM STONED BY THE
CHIPPEWAS—LODGES AND CANOES OF THE CHIPPEWAS—A
NARROW ESCAPE FROM A WATERY GRAVE—"COME IN THE
HOUSE AND SEE US"—BRAINERD—I RETURN TO MY HOME—
TOLEDO, CLEVELAND, ERIE, READING AND HARRISBURG—
A WHITE WOMAN'S CAPTIVITY AMONG THE INDIANS—THEY
COMPEL HER TO JOIN THEM IN THEIR WARS AGAINST THE
WHITES—THE DEADLY TOMAHAWK—SHE DROWNS A SQUAW
AND THEN ESCAPES—THE ST. LAWRENCE—OGDENSBURG—
THE CANADIANS—ONWARD—DAVENPORT AND DES MOINES—
HISTORY OF THE SIOUX INDIANS—A VOCABULARY OF THEIR
LANGUAGE, AND NAMES OF THEIR CHIEFS TRANSLATED:

REACHING Bismarck, I remained a few days, and
then started for Brainerd, Minnesota, a small town
situated on the Mississippi River, about a hundred
and fifty miles from its source.

Bismarck is situated on a fine prairie, about two
miles from the Missouri River. It does a lucrative
trade with the Black Hills, the military posts and

Indian agencies. At the time of my visit the town was in its infancy, and like all border towns, it was often the scene of strife and bloodshed.

The *Tribune*, now a journal of power and influence, had been started but a few weeks before, and occupied a little frame shanty, through the crevices of which, it was not difficult to see daylight.

Calling at a lawyer's office, a log hut, intending to have a chat with the proprietor about affairs in general, I found the legal gentleman lying upon the office-floor, the prairie sod, sound asleep, while the client's chair, a huge buffalo skull, was lying in one corner of the hut, as though there was not a land-contest to be settled. I let him sleep undisturbed.

The country traversed by the Northern Pacific Railroad, in Dakota, between the Missouri and the Red River of the North, is grand and beautiful. For a distance of forty miles, in some places, the track lies upon what appears to be a perfect level. These tracts stretch in every direction, and the eye is lost in a halo of dreamy and ethereal space as it endeavors to penetrate their dimensions.

In summer time, the face of the country appears like a sea of green, waving billows, the sameness of which, is occasionally relieved by small groves and belts of cotton-wood which border the creeks, that in the distance, appear like huge, shining serpents winding through the tall grass.

When these beautiful prairies of Dakota become

more generally known, thousands of emigrants will seek no further for farms and homes after they enter upon their lovely, productive surface.

One morning, when about fourteen miles west of Brainerd, I noticed several Chippewa Indians a few rods ahead of me. They soon began to stone me, but as they were right in my course, I walked on, managing to dodge all the stones they threw. As soon as I reached them, they searched my pockets, and tried to take my revolver, but I held it in my hand ready for action, so they concluded to let me retain it.

Only one of them was armed, his weapon being an old muzzle-loading shot gun. I requested him to let me examine it, which he did. I then made him understand that I wanted to discharge it and see if it was a good gun. At this he became very angry, and told me that he had but one gun-cap.

I knew if that cap was off the gun, he would be harmless, but with it on, he would likely use it, in order to get my clothes and pistol, and then sink my body in one of the neighboring lakes. So I removed the cap from the tube, and dropped it into the sand, and while pretending to look for it, I was careful to tramp it deeper.

They all became enraged at this, but there was no remedy, and suddenly changing their demeanor, they invited me to accompany them to their lodges in the forest; but I declined to do it, after which I proceeded on my way, and they soon after disappeared among the pines.

A few miles further on, I noticed a smoke in the timber, and upon going up to it, I found a small Chippewa camp. The only occupants at the time, were a little Indian girl and a young baby. As soon as the little squaw espied me, she began to cry lustily, and picking up the baby, ran away and hid in some bushes.

Being unable to speak a word of the Chippewa language, I could not convince the child that I was harmless, so I continued on my way.

I soon reached two other camps in the woods, where I found the Indians living in tents made of birch-bark. Several of the women were dressing deer skins and making moccasins, while the braves were playing a game of chance, which very much resembled the white man's game of billiards.

For a table they used a blanket spread upon the ground, and for balls they substituted rifle bullets, while their ramrods served as cues.

These Indians had huckle-berries in abundance, standing about in birch-bark baskets, and minus sugar and cream, I had a luxury delicious and refreshing. As I left the camp, I noticed an Indian scalp near one of the lodges, which I supposed had been taken in a fight with the Sioux, some time before, as small bands of both tribes occasionally get together, when a battle is the result.

In a beautiful grove of pines, on the bank of the Mississippi, I visited a large camp of Chippewas, and was kindly entertained by them. They had secured a young pig in one of the settlements, and after removing the bristles, pierced it through and through with a pointed stake, and then suspended it over a fire to roast, laying the stake which held the pig, across the top of two forked posts.

A fine old chief invited me to remain and join them at the feast, but not admiring the manner in which they had dressed the pig, I declined. After that, when traveling among the Indians, a lack of cleanliness in the cooking arrangements was not a great source of inconvenience to my appetite, for hunger and an open-air life, created a relish for food that untidiness in cooking could not remove.

During the summer months, these Indians subsist principally upon fish, wild ducks and berries, all of which abound in Minnesota. In the fall and winter, they gather large quantities of hazel-nuts, and hunt deer, bears and other game.

The Chippewas make their lodges out of birch-bark, instead of skins, as most Indians do. Their canoes, baskets and other implements of general use, are constructed of the same material.

The light birch-bark canoe is to the Chippewa as useful and necessary a means of transportation and travel, in his land of lakes and rivers, as the Indian pony is to the Sioux of the prairie.

The women and children, like the warriors, are expert with the canoe, and it is wonderful how rapidly they can propel it through the water with a small paddle. A bark canoe that will hold three persons, is so light, that a squaw will carry it for miles on her head.

The Chippewas of Northern Minnesota are divided into bands, known as the Leech Lake, Rabbit Lake, Red Lake and Gull Lake bands. The chiefs of the different bands are Bad Boy, Crossing Sky and Big Dog.

One day, while alone on the bank of the Mississippi, I resolved to try my skill at paddling one of the Indian canoes which I found there, the owners, at the time, being absent. I soon had the craft in the water, but the instant I stepped into it, over it went, bottom side up, and throwing me head first into the river, which was deep at the very brink.

I could not swim an inch, and how I got out, I can not to this day conceive. A strange, indescribable influence seemed to control me, and without knowing by what means, I reached the shore.

I remember going down twice, and it seemed a long, long time before I reached the bottom, and then again arose to the surface. Like a flash my childhood days came to my mind, and I fancied I could see my mother at home, and hear her voice as plain as I ever did.

My escape from a watery grave was miraculous,

but He who watches over all, willed it so, and to Him I owe my grateful homage.

After reaching the bank, and drawing the canoe out of the water, I proceeded to Brainerd, drenched thoroughly, and resolving to meddle no more with an Indian bark canoe. On entering the town, Mr. Frank Russel, a resident of the place, who was sitting on the piazza of his house, began a conversation with me, addressing me about as follows:

"Well, stranger, how do you find roving these days? I spent sixteen years at it before I married and settled down, and I know something about it. Come in the house and see us! The 'latch-string' at my house always hangs on the outside for the rover, and my wife has a warm place in her heart for the traveler far from home."

When I last heard of Mr. Russel, he was doing well, and was an engineer on the Wisconsin Central Railroad.

There is a time, I believe, when the ardor of all roving dispositions grows cold, and longs for home life and its comforts. A young "brother printer," in North Carolina, gave me a hint in the following language, as near as I now remember:

"A man never knows what happiness, comfort and contentment are, until he settles down, secures a good, sensible wife, has a sweet little child to pet when he goes home, and a rocking-chair and a pair of easy slippers to rest in."

Brainerd is one of the prettiest towns, of the kind, I ever visited. It is a forest town, and is entirely surrounded by grand old pines; even in the streets and private yards, are to be seen the tall, straight, evergreen sentinels.

The streets resemble well-regulated parks more than business thoroughfares. The pleasant aroma of the pines is ever present, and there is a pleasing contrast between the cozy white dwellings and the green foliage, which are so closely mingled.

Brainerd is a trading point for the Chippewas, and nearly every day, there are some of them in the town. In winter, they bring in game and furs, and during the summer, they sell berries, fish and birch-bark baskets.

Leaving Minnesota, I started for Philadelphia, going by way of Chicago, Toledo, Cleveland, Erie and Reading.

Toledo, on Maumee River, four miles from Lake Erie, is one of the best lake harbors, and is largely engaged in shipping and commerce.

Cleveland, like Toledo, is a lake port, and a ship-building point. The city contains many factories, and is a prominent railroad center.

Erie, on Lake Erie, is the only lake town of importance in Pennsylvania. It is a busy, thriving city, and does a large trade in coal and oil.

Reading, Pennsylvania, is situated on the Schuyl-kill, fifty-two miles above Philadelphia, and is the

center of a fine farming district.   The residents of
this locality, are known as the "Pennsylvania Germans," who are the descendants of the Germans
by whom that section of country was first settled.
These people are noted for their generosity, and
quiet, plain mode of life.

After remaining a short time in Philadelphia, I
went to Harrisburg, where I obtained a situation
on the *Temperance Blessing*, published by Mr. C. L.
Boyer.   Here I remained for six months, and then
went to Canada, but returned to Pennsylvania a
short time after.

Harrisburg, the capital of Pennsylvania, is finely
situated on the Susquehanna, and is surrounded
by beautiful river and mountain scenery.   On the
river's bank, facing the city, is the grave of John
Harris, after whom the city was named.   The grave
is inclosed by a neat iron fence, and the old trunk
of a huge and ancient tree, to which the Indians
had bound Harris, and then attempted to torture
him, is also within the inclosure.

About the year 1745, my father's grandmother,
Barbara Haehnlen, then a little girl seven years of
age, was captured by the Indians, on the Susquehanna, near where Harrisburg now stands.   Both
of her parents, and one little sister, were killed.
The Indians bent to the ground two young trees,
and after tying the child to them, allowed them to
fly apart, thus tearing her to pieces.

The little girl was then placed in a canoe with several Indians, and taken to the opposite shore. A storm prevailed at the time, and the child being bound and helpless, was exposed to its fury until an old squaw covered her with a blanket.

As she grew older, the Indians compelled her to join them in their wars against the whites, and in one of their battles she received shot in her arm that could never be safely removed. During one of their fights with the settlers she drew a tomahawk from a white man's skull, where it had been thrown with unerring aim by one of the Indians. For this act she came very near losing her life.

On one occasion, after the captive had been a number of years with the Indians, and while helping a squaw to wash some clothes on the bank of a stream, she suddenly pushed her into the water, and then struck her on the head and arms with a club until she sank. Running to the village, some distance away, she informed the Indians that the squaw had fallen into the river.

Taking advantage of the excitement occasioned by this report, the captive escaped. For several days she secreted herself in a hollow tree, that was surrounded by water. The Indians followed her so closely that, at times, she could hear them talk, and once their dogs went up to the tree, but did not discover her, as she had thrown them off her trail by wading in the water.

When the savages left for camp, she crept from her hiding place, and after a long and wearisome journey through the wilderness, reached the white settlements, having been in captivity about twenty years. She subsequently married, and her children and grandchildren would often gather about the huge, old-fashioned fireplace, during the long winter evenings, to hear her relate her adventures while a captive among the Indians.

She died in 1822, then a gray-headed woman upwards of eighty years of age, and her ashes rest in the old cemetery at Petersburg, Lancaster County, Pennsylvania.

Reaching Ogdensburg, New York, on my way to Canada, I crossed the St. Lawrence to Prescott, on the Canadian side, and from there I proceeded to Brockville by way of the Grand Trunk Railway.

Although it was the month of March, and the weather was intensely cold, the river was open for navigation. The St. Lawrence, owing to its great depth, seldom closes entirely, even during severe winters. It is a magnificent river, and on account of its vastness, and the blue color of its waters, it resembles the lakes, of which it is the outlet.

Ogdensburg is one of the most northern towns in the state of New York, and is a prominent point for travel and traffic between the United States and the British Provinces.

The Canadians are a hearty, vigorous people, and

love their country. The ladies are plump and rosy, good-natured and sensible, and wear thick, woolen stockings and fur-caps.

A few months after my return from Canada, I made a tour to the Indian country of Dakota, by way of Chicago, Davenport, Des Moines and Fort Dodge.

Davenport, on the Mississippi, at the foot of the Upper Rapids, is a fine city, and a great lumber market. On Rock Island, opposite the city, is the Central Armory of the United States.

Des Moines, the capital of Iowa, is situated on the river which bears its name, and is one of the largest and most flourishing cities in the state.

The Indians I visited were the Yankton Sioux, and their camp was pleasantly located on the north bank of the Missouri, sixty miles above the city of Yankton, and thirty miles below Fort Randall.

In the early days of America, when the white settlements were confined to the Atlantic Coast, the Sioux Indians occupied what is now the states of Wisconsin, Minnesota and Iowa, but within the last half century they have been principally identified with localities further west. Father Alloue, a Catholic priest, who visited a tribe of the nation on the shore of Lake Superior, in 1665, was in all probability, the first white man who ever ventured to form the acquaintance of the Sioux.

In 1766, Captain Jonathan Carver, a bold and

resolute traveler, made a lengthy tour among the
Sioux Indians of the then unexplored interior of
North America. He passed the winter of that year
among the Sioux, near Big Stone Lake, which now
forms a part of the line between Minnesota and
Dakota. He visited the Red Pipe-stone Quarry
with the Indians, during his sojourn among them,
and as he probably was the first white man to see
the Sioux Mecca, the stone would be more justly
known as Carverite, instead of Catlinite.

Those fearless, devoted Indian travelers, Catlin
and Schoolcraft, men who spent much time and
money traveling among the American Aborigines,
probably obtained a far better knowledge of their
general manners and customs, than any other men
who ever mingled among these strange, interesting
people of the forests and plains.

The Sioux were once known as "Naudowessie,"
but within the last century they have assumed the
present appellation, which they claim was given by
white men. There are over twelve different tribes
in the Sioux Nation, among which the principal are
the Unkpapa, Ogalalla, Brule, Yankton, Titonwan,
Minneconjon and Saus Arcs.

I append a short lexicon of the Sioux language.
The words are spelled according to the sound in
pronouncing them, and I insert only nouns, as the
Indian names of objects will probably be the most
interesting to the reader.

Arrow—We-hink-pe. Antelope—Tah-to-kah-dahn.
Ax—Un-spah. Ant—Tah-jus-kah.
Buffalo—Tah-ton-kah. Book—Wo-wah-pe.
Bow—E-tah-ze-po. Baby—Ho-ke-she-yo-pah.
Bed—O-win-ja. Bag—Wo-ju-hah. Bear—Mah-to.
Ball—Tah-pah. Bark—Cahn-hah. Blood—We-ah.
Bead—Wahn-ah-pin. Beard—Pu-tin-hah.
Beaver—Cah-pah. Bed—O-wahn-kah.
Bird—Zit-kah-dahn. Boat—Wah-tah.
Bone—Hu-hu. Buckskin—Tah-hah.
Cannon—Mah-zah-kan-ton-kah. Chin—E-ko.
Canoe—Cahn-wah-to. Captive—Wy-ah-kah.
Cat—Enmu-shun-kah. Cave—Mah-cor-do-kahn.
Chicken—Ahn-pah-hoto-nah. Chief—To-kah-pah.
Coffee—Pe-ju-ta-sap-pah. Corn—Wahm-ne-he-zah.
Deer—Tock-cah. Dew—Coo. Dog—Shun-kah.
Eagle—Wahn-me-dee. Elk—Her-ah-kah.
Ear—No-gee. Earth—Mah-gah. Eye—Ish-tah.
Fire—Pa-tah. Face—E-tee. Father—Ah-tee.
Feast—Wo-tah-pe. Friend—Ko-dah.
God—Wah-kahn-ton-kah. Gun—Mah-zah-kin.
Husband—He-nah-coo. , Horse—Shunk-ton-kah.
Heart—Tah-cahn-tah. Home—Te-yah-tah.
House—Te-pee. Hand—Nah-pee. Hill—Pah-hah.
Island—We-tah. Ice—Cah-gah. Iron—Mah-zah.
Jar—Mah-kah,che-gah. Joint—O-ke-hee.
Knife—Me-nah. Knee—Hu-pah-hu.
Lake—Me-dee. Lead—**Mah-zah-zu.**
Lasso—We-kahn. Leggin—Hun-skah.

Man----We-cash-ah.   Mother----E-nah.   Moose----Ta.
Medicine----Pe-je-hu-tah.   Meat----Tah-do.
Nose----Po-gee.   Neck----Tah-hu.   Nest----Ho-pee.
Opossum----He-tonk-tahn-kah.   Onion----Pe-shin.
Paddle----Wahm-nah-hee-ah.   Pig----Ku-cush.
Pain----Woy·ah-zahn.   Path----Cahn-cor.
Pine----Wah-ze-cahn.   Prairie----Tin-tah.
Quail----Pah-win-jah.   Quarry----In-yan-o-gah-pe.
River----Wock-pah-dahn.   Rabbit----Mosh-ten-cah.
Sister----Tunk-she.   Salt----Min-is ku-yah.
Skull----Pah-hu-hu.   Sky----Mock-pe-ah.   ·
Smoke----So-tah.   Snow----Wah.   Sun----Wee.
Spoon----Tu-ke-kah.   Star----We-chop-pee.
Scalp----We-cah-pah.   Song----O-do-wan.
Tomahawk----Onspe-cahn-pe-dahn.   Teeth----Hee.
Tobacco----Cahn-dee.   Tongue----Che-pee.
Uncle----Deck-she.   Under-clothes----Mah-hen-unpe.
Vine----We-yo-we.   Valley----Os-mah-kah.
Water----Minne.   Water-fall----Minne-hah-hah.
Yesterday----Nah-ahn-hin.   Youth----Kash-kah.

I give the following translations of Sioux names according to the Indian method of arranging the words· of a sentence, which is, in many cases, the reverse of the English mode. Thus the English version of "Mock-pe-ah Alu-tah," would become "Cloud Red."

In the general construction of the language, the Sioux name the noun first, followed by the qualifying words, and the verb last.

Sitting Bull—Tah-ton-kah O-tah-kah.

Red Cloud—Mock-pe-ah Alu-tah.

Spotted Tail—Sinte E-lish-kah.

Long Dog—Shun-kah Han-skah.

Broad Trail—Cahn-coo Ton-kah.

Pretty Bear—Mah-to Wash-ta.

Little Knife—Me-nah Chis-te-nah.

Cloud Horn—Pe-te-he Mock-pe-ah.

Standing Elk—Her-ah-kah Nah-zin.

Spotted Eagle—Wahn-me-dee E-lish-kah.

Medicine Lake—Me-dee Pe-ju-tah.

Bellowing Buffalo—Tah-ton-kah Ho-ton.

Fast Dog—Shun-kah Lu-zah.

Long Pumpkin—Wahn-nu Han-skah.

Painted Face—E-tee Sam-yah.

High Shield—Wah-cahn-kah Han-skah.

Standing Bear—Mah-to Nah-zin.

Two Strike—No-pah Gosh-pah.

Crazy Horse—Shunk-ton-kah He-nah-she-kin-yahn.

Man-Afraid-of-His-Horses——Shunk-ton-kah-Tah-wa-
e-tahn-kahn-Ko-ke-pah-We-cash-ah.

CHAPTER XI.

No friendly roof—no home,
No light from open doors at evening greeting
Our weary coming—no fond, happy meeting,
No matter where we roam,
No home.

No quiet, peaceful hearth
Round which the little ones with faces bright
May smile and prattle, in the cheerful light,
In innocence and mirth,
No home.

ANON.

I FIND A WHITE FEMALE MISSIONARY LIVING ALONE AMONG THE SIOUX—THE SCALP DANCE—A SAVAGE SCENE—DEATH OF AN INDIAN CHILD—I AM DETECTED WHILE EXAMINING AN INDIAN GRAVE—HOW I WON THE FRIENDSHIP OF THE INDIANS—HOME AGAIN—MY EXPERIENCE AS A PUBLISHER—NOT YET WEARY OF TRAVELING—A FRIENDLY ENGINEER—STERLING, MADISON AND PORTAGE CITY—HOW THE SIOUX DEMOLISH A PRINTING OFFICE—SIOUX FALLS—THE INDIAN PIPE-STONE QUARRY—MY IDEAL HOME—THE AUTHOR OF "SWEET HOME"—THOUGHTS—A DESERTED HUT, AND WHAT I FOUND THERE—A SCANT DINNER—I MOVE SOUTHWARD—KANSAS CITY, FORT SCOTT, TOPEKA AND LINCOLN—ON THE PRAIRIES—SUFFERING FOR WATER—THOUGHTS OF MOTHER—NIOBRARA—I FIND A LITTLE WHITE GIRL HELD CAPTIVE BY THE SIOUX INDIANS.

AFTER spending a few days with the Yanktons, I started for a Ponca village, located twenty miles further down the Missouri, near the mouth of the Ponca. Walking all day through the Sioux camps, which were scattered along the river for a distance of about fifteen miles, I reached Choteau Creek. Here the Sioux informed me that a white lady was living among them and teaching their children.

I was much surprised to hear this, and resolved to call upon the lady. Proceeding to her dwelling, a comfortable log hut, I was received courteously, and with no little surprise, for a white face was not an everyday sight in that locality.

I found this missionary to be Miss Louise Buchannan, of Michigan, who had been sent among the Sioux as a teacher, by the Episcopal Church. For several years previous, she had been laboring in Northern Minnesota among the Chippewas.

She was highly educated and accomplished, and had a fine library, which must have been a source of comfort and company to her, shut out as she was, from civilization.

She had a log school-house near her dwelling, in which the Sioux children received the primary elements of an education. About five hundred Sioux were living within half a mile of her house, but so thoroughly had she gained their love and respect, that she lived in their midst without fear or molestation. The men would never enter the dwelling without being invited to do so, and when calling upon some errand concerning their children, they would transact the business at the door.

I passed the night at the house of the estimable teacher, as also did an Indian family who were her

particularly trusted Sioux friends.   We had a nice
supper, and with the exception of the conduct of
one of the little Indian boys, who wanted to eat
New York jelly with his fingers, the affair passed
off as pleasantly as though we had been in a civilized community.

The lady has since married and left the Mission.
I trust the reader joins me in wishing that, in her
new mission, the same kindness and respect may
be her reward that crowned her labors among the
Sioux· Indians.

The next morning I crossed the Missouri with
an Indian, in a canoe, and then proceeded to the
Ponca Indian camp, about five miles distant.   The
first night I witnessed a scalp-dance, which had
been brought about in this wise: Several Brules
from Spotted Tail's village, then on White Earth
River, had been shot while stealing ponies near the
Ponca village, and as the two tribes are hereditary
enemies, a scalp-dance was the result.

The bloody scalps, hands and arms of the dead
Sioux, were placed upon poles erected for the purpose, and after this was done, the exalting Ponca
warriors assembled to perform the dance, adorned
and painted in the most frightful manner.   Some
were partly covered with buffalo hides, beneath
which, the hideously painted and distorted face,
only half revealed by the flickering blaze of the
council-fire, presented a terribly wild picture.

A number of braves formed in a circle around
the poles to which the scalps had been fastened.
Inside the circle of warriors was a fire, over which
were hanging several huge pots containing dogs'
meat.   About three hundred Indians took part in
the ceremony, all jumping and stamping with such
power, as to shake the ground beneath them.

As usual, on such occasions, they made the most
outlandish gestures, and assumed the wildest and
most uncouth attitudes imaginable, all the while
shouting the fearful war-hoop, and striking toward
each other with their weapons as though they were
the most deadly enemies.   At intervals of about
twenty minutes, they all stopped dancing, and seat-
ing themselves upon the ground, cross-legged, each
one was served with a dishful of the dogs' meat by
old men who officiated as waiters.

The chief, after disposing of his portion, made a
short speech, and then resumed his seat, when the
Indians arose and began to dance again.   Soon the
yelling and leaping would grow more furious and
faster, and as they became still more excited, their
glittering, snake-like, black eyes protruded with a
fiendish, indescribable appearance, as they gnashed
their teeth, and by simultaneous sounds, tried to
imitate the sibilant, gurgling sound of the death-
struggles of their victims.

The scene was shocking in the extreme, as the
gory scalps were held aloft in the light of the fire,

and the half naked and reeling forms were dimly visible by the faint glow of the dying blaze.

This ceremony is generally performed at night, consequently its terrible characteristics are greatly heightened by the weird glare of the glimmering fire. They always end these dances by fierce barks and yelps, resembling that of savage dogs.

The next morning an Indian child died in the village, and there was much weeping and lamenting among the relations. The chief made a consolatory speech to the parents of the deceased child.

While with these Indians I endeavored to examine some graves, but I was so closely watched that I never succeeded in the undertaking. One time, when about to climb upon a scaffold containing an embalmed body, a slight rustle in the bushes near by attracted my attention, and a moment after a party of squaws confronted me, and in an excited manner, bade me leave the spot at once, before the warriors could discover me. Upon going to the camp, I did not learn that the squaws had said any thing to the men about it.

The Poncas were kind and friendly, and in the heat of excitement, when they were engaged in the scalp-dance, and when I 'was the only white man in all that savage band, they invited me to a seat in their midst, requested me to join them at their feast of dogs' meat, and were as respectful to me as though they were in sight of Fort Randall.

When nearing an Indian camp that I had never visited before, I assumed an air of boldness and self-possession that was often difficult to do. An unconcerned and fearless demeanor is greatly admired and respected by the Indians.

When with the Sioux, I could find friends and "make myself at home" in any village I entered. The idea of a solitary white man walking right into their midst, and speaking their own language, at once won their confidence and protection. Of course, when a traveler "is in Rome, he does as the Romans do," as far as it is policy to do so. I could sit on the ground, cross-legged, with them, eat out of the same dish, smoke the pipe when it was passed around, sleep upon their fur-beds, ride their ponies, use the bow and arrows, accompany them to their councils and dances, and lastly, but not the least feature in my method of pleasing them, I could pet their dogs and babies.

So long as a man can find favor in the eyes of the ladies and the babies, he is on the safe side, be he in a Sioux camp or a civilized domicile, and the men will be only in the background. This is logic that few will deny.

Leaving the Poncas, I started for the town of Niobrara, but upon reaching the Running Water, or Niobrara River, eleven miles from the Indian camp, I found that I could not ford it. Some of the Ponca tribe had a village on this stream, but had deserted it a few days before through fear of the raiding Sioux.

As I could not wade the river on account of the treacherous beds of quick-sand, of which its bottom is mostly formed, I returned to the main camp of the Poncas, and there crossed the Missouri, then going to Sioux City instead of Niobrara. Continuing eastward, I arrived at home in due season, in September, 1874.

Here I commenced the manufacture and sale of several little domestic articles, and the publication of some household recipes, in which I was successful, and I found the business to be a very valuable means of educating myself in business habits, and the ways of the world generally. Next I purchased a printing-office and published the first edition of this work, a little pamphlet of fifty-four pages. It was well received by the public, and the issue was exhausted in a few months. A second edition was then printed, and it met with a like reception.

I was not then weary of traveling, as I now am, and, after arranging my affairs at home, and going to see the Centennial Exhibition, at Philadelphia, I started for the West. Reaching Bellaire, Ohio, I met Mr. F. Trembly, an engineer on the Baltimore and Ohio Railroad, with whom I rode to Monroe-ville, two hundred miles distant. He was a very friendly, courteous young man, and I had a pleasant ride on his iron-horse.

At Rock Falls, Illinois, I secured a position on the *Progress*, and while in this office I formed the acquaintance of Dr. H. C. Clements, a physician of Sterling, Illinois, and a genial, warm-hearted man. I remember both the Doctor and his good lady with kindness and respect.

Sterling is an attractive little city handsomely located on Rock River, opposite Rock Falls, and one hundred and ten miles west of Chicago. It is the home of many former Pennsylvanians.

In a few months, I went to Wisconsin, and from there to St. Paul and Minneapolis; thence to Elk Point, Dakota, by way of Mankato and Sioux City.

From Beloit, Wisconsin, I rode up to Madison on a passenger-train locomotive, by permission of Mr. James Hecox, the gentlemanly engineer.

Madison, the capital of Wisconsin, is situated between Lakes Mendota and Monona. During the summer the lakes are a favorite resort for boating and fishing, and in the winter the novel sport of gliding over their frozen surface in sail-sleighs, is enjoyed by the people.

From Madison I went to Lodi, then across the country to Portage City. This is a pretty place, located on the Wisconsin River, near the site of old Fort Winnebago.

Reaching St. Paul, I met Mr. George Dyer, an old school-mate, who had located in the city a few years before and gone into business.

At Minneapolis I was employed awhile in the printing establishment of Judd & Company, after which I went to Dakota. From Elk Point I continued on to Sioux Falls, a frontier town situated one hundred miles distant, on the Sioux River.

This journey I performed alone, and on foot, over one of the most enchanting prairie districts the sun ever shone upon. I enjoyed the trip very much, rough and lonesome as it was, for in being surrounded by the beauties of Nature, not yet at the mercy of civilization's blighting hands, I ever found pleasure and enjoyment not to be obtained within the pale of civilization.

The town of Sioux Falls is pleasantly located on the site of the old fort whose name it bears, and almost within hearing of the leaping, roaring, foaming Sioux Falls, the sight of which is partly obstructed by the timber growing upon an island in the river just above the cataract.

Here I secured a situation on the *Independent*, also on the *Pantagraph*, and remained until the desire to move on prompted me to lay aside the labors of the printing-office, and seek the air and attractions of the outer world.

Shortly after the town was laid out, and when it contained that magic institution of civilization and progress—a printing-office—the place was raided by the Sioux Indians. They broke the press into pieces, melted the type together for the purpose of making pipes, and "pied" the material generally.

What the poor editor and printers did, I know not, but it is safe to suppose that the savages saw in these over-worked, poorly-paid knights of the "quill and stick," nothing to excite fear; and if they faithfully promised the Sioux that they would never join the "Indian ring," or support in their future papers, the present defective and dishonest "Indian policy," their lives were probably spared.

About a mile from the town, the Sioux River, a very quiet prairie stream, suddenly awakens from its wonted lethargy and calmness, and nearing a succession of massive red boulders, becomes one dashing, whirling, roaring body of spray and foam, and, with a tremendous, rushing sound, leaps over the rocky chasms, thus forming the picturesque, romantic and fascinating Sioux Falls.

The falls were a favorite resort of the Indians from time immemorial, and even since the whites have encroached upon their lands and rights, they visit the locality.

From this place I went up to the Sioux Indian Red Pipe Stone Quarry, about fifty miles distant. It is situated in southwestern Minnesota, several miles from the Dakota line. My route, for forty miles, lay over a very beautiful prairie country, in close proximity to the Sioux River, then leaving that stream, I reached the quarry by traveling ten or twelve miles due east.

The traveler approaching this quarry from the west, reaches Pipe-stone Creek soon after leaving the Sioux River, of which the creek is a tributary. The water is cool and delicious, and so clear that every fish and pebble can be distinctly seen upon the bottom. At this stream I found the deserted camp of a hunting or trapping party.

The quarry is about one mile in length, and less than one sixteenth of a mile in width. Lying, as it does, upon one side of a bluff, it can be seen for miles before reaching it, and at a distance, owing to the innumerable juttings and irregular excavations made by the Indians while procuring their pipe-stone, it resembles an Indian camp with singular and striking similarity.

The stone is taken out of the quarry in layers from one to two inches thick. It is very easy to carve, and is susceptible of a fine polish. Most of the stone is of a dark red color, but sometimes a layer of a lighter shade is found, which is often beautifully variegated with white and yellow spots and streaks.

Some geographical writers, who, perhaps, were unwilling to walk two hundred miles through the wilderness to see the quarry, erroneously describe it and its contents as a bank of red clay, out of which the Indians get the material to make their sun-baked pipes. But the substance is a species of magnesian mineral, and resembles soap-stone.

Regarding the formation of this stone, there are two traditions current among the Sioux. One of them is that, at the time of the Flood, all the bad Sioux were washed to the spot and turned into this stone. The other account is that, many years ago, the Sioux and the Chippewas had a battle on the present site of the quarry, and the blood that was shed sank into the ground and formed into red stone.

For centuries the Sioux have secured stone for making pipes at this place, and they guard it with jealous care and never allow other Indians to visit it, though they willingly sell them pipes. Once a year, a delegation of Indians from various tribes of the Sioux nation journey to the quarry for the purpose of worship, and in order to secure some of the supposed sacred stone.

The ground at the quarry is always strewn with bones, and other remains of banquets held by the Indians when on their pilgrimage to the place.

Near the foot of the quarry are three immense circular-shaped rocks, which are known to hunters and bordermen as "The Three Maidens." They are close together, and are the only rocks of the kind for miles around. The Indians say that a young warrior committed suicide by leaping from the top of one of the rocks to the ground below, on account of some heart-trouble, for which, as is generally the case, a maiden was to blame.

In the spring and early summer, there are three beautiful streams of water which flow through the quarry, and leaping through the huge cavities, and over the red stone, form lovely and picturesque torrents and water-falls.

The prairie scenery in the vicinity is grand and enchanting. The beauty which has endeared this section of country to the hearts of the Sioux for many generations, will be the means of alluring the ever-intruding white man.

From the quarry I walked to the settlement of Luverne, about thirty miles distant, and carried a portion of the stone with me, out of which I will have made a pipe-stone top center-table, if I ever become so fortunate as to sail into that harbor of peace, contentment, and shelter from the storms of life's buffeting elements, namely, a happy, comfortable home of my own.

The event of my settling down was frequently a subject of thought, and I always looked forward to the time with pleasure. Many times have I, as I walked along the streets of some city or village, stopped before a dwelling to observe, by the aid of the evening lamp, my ideal home-scene.

Perhaps around the table were the mother and little ones (two is the limit to my idea of the number of little ones), sewing, reading, or engaged in some parlor-game, while the husband, home from the labors of the day, occupied an easy chair, as he read in silence, or aloud, the news of the day or the contents of some favorite book.

If a sweet, rosy, dimpled little baby was creeping about the floor, trying to catch the cat, poking the fire, or engaged in some other baby pranks, and a melodeon occupied a place in the room, as well as the pictures and other little adornments that should grace the home, my ideal was perfect.

The reader, should he or she be a married man or woman, may possibly deem me unjust for not giving the mother-in-law a prominent place in the happy home-scene; but the dear old lady was at a neighbor's house complaining about her son-in-law, and telling how much better catnip-tea was made, and babies managed when she was young, so she passed from my mind.

A great and good writer once declared that one hour of domestic happiness was worth more than a lifetime of pleasure found in business, wealth or any other channel.

If my imagination has soard too high into the realms of fancy, the reader will surely admit that even a poor printer is entitled to live in a castle, though it be merely in the air.

How sad to know that J. Howard Payne, the author of the beautiful and immortal song, known in every civilized land as *Home, Sweet Home*, was a homeless wanderer. He was inspired with the idea of this soul-stirring melody while walking the streets of London, wondering where he would get food and lodging.

He once informed a correspondent that after he composed the lines that had been forced out of his heart by absolute want of a home, and when their melody had become familiar to every soul, he often found himself wandering through the streets of some great city, without a shilling to pay for a dinner, or a place to lay his head; and that, too, while he could see, through the half-open window-blinds of some comfortable home, a happy family circle who were singing the popular song in joyful strains, unconscious of the fact that the author of their song, who was a penniless, heart-broken man, was looking upon them.

This man, an American, never had a home, and he once informed a friend that he desired to die in a foreign country, and be buried by strangers. At last, the United States Government appointed him Consul at Tunis, where he died in 1852.

On my way to Luverne I had a rough journey over bluffs and through sloughs, and a very fierce prairie storm prevailed all the time. When about half-way to the settlement, I came to an old log hut. It had been deserted by the owners, and the only occupant I found, was a forlorn-looking owl, which screeched hideously when I climbed in the cabin, in order to get a handful of wheat which I noticed in one corner.

Putting some of the grain in my hat, and taking an old can, that had done service as a candle-stick, I started to a neighboring slough for some water, after which I sat down upon the ground to dine. This is what Mark Twain calls "roughing it," and it is a type of a traveler's experience in the wilds of the far West.

From Luverne I proceeded southward, passing through Sioux City, St. Joseph and Kansas City. After a short stay at Fort Scott, Kansas, I visited Parsons, Neosho Falls, Burlington, Junction City, Lawrence and Topeka, and worked at the printing business at different points along the way.

Kansas City, on the Missouri, is the largest and most important place between the Mississippi and the Pacific Ocean. It is a marvelous mart of trade and business commotion, and is the center of a net-work of railroads. Steamboat communication with all Missouri, Mississippi and Ohio River ports is also enjoyed by this rising metropolis.

Fort Scott is a pretty, growing town, and bids fair to become an important point. It is a place of trade for a wide scope of farming country. Fort Scott coal has secured a reputation in the West for quality and quantity.

Topeka, said to mean "big potato" in one of the Indian languages, is the capital of Kansas, and is located on the Kansas River. From here I went to Lincoln, the capital of Nebraska.

This is a very thriving, energetic, young capital, finely located in a beautiful prairie region. It is a railroad center, and a grain market of importance.

While in Lincoln I was engaged in the printing and publishing house of Robinson & Hyde, and after fulfilling my engagement with the firm, I started for Niobrara, on the Missouri River, about one hundred and fifty miles north of Lincoln.

This journey I performed on foot, as there were no railroads to that place, but the scenery on the way amply rewarded me for the fatiguing march.

After crossing the Platte River, my course was through the beautiful Elkhorn Valley, which a few years ago, was the hunting-ground of the Omaha. Pawnee and Ponca Indians.

While walking across the prairie near Elkhorn River, I found a very large stone tomahawk, such as were used by the Indians before they could get iron. It must have been used only on special occasions, and it was so heavy that I was obliged to leave it behind, much as I desired to possess it.

Between Neligh and Niobrara, a distance of fifty miles, the country was then but sparsely settled, and I did not see a house in half a day's travel. The heat was very oppressive, and I walked thirty miles before reaching water, so that my suffering from thirst became severe.

I had missed the regular trail, or I would have found water long before I did. Several times I became exhausted, and lying down in the grass, I hoped to find relief in its cooling shade.

Reader, unless you have traveled on the plains of the 'West, under a scorching sun, without water, you can have but a faint idea of the agony brought on by such experience.

In my misery my thoughts went back to my far-distant home, and to my kind, gentle mother. We seldom realize a mother's love and worth until by death, or some other cause, she has been placed far beyond our reach, and her voice of love and sympathy no longer greets our ears.

At last, I noticed a flock of birds hovering over a little meadow, between some undulating table-land, and upon going to the place as fast as my limbs would carry me, I found a pool of dark, brackish water, sheltered from the sun's rays by the high grass that grew in its shallow bed.

With a heart full of thankfulness to the Giver of all, I quenched my thirst, and then pushed on. In a little while, faint and ill, I reached a dwelling, in which I was kindly received and cared for by the inmates, the family of a Mr. James Anderson.

The next day I reached Niobrara, and accepted a position on the *Pioneer*, the official organ of the Northwestern military posts and Indian agencies, published by Messrs. Fry & Draper.

Niobrara is advantageously situated on a grand prairie, at the confluence of the Missouri and Niobrara Rivers, and is the seat of the United States Land Office of Knox County, which district comprises some of the most beautiful and inviting land in the West.

Niobrara is forty miles above Yankton, and as it is the last town on the Central Black Hills Route, it has become a popular outfitting point for miners, travelers and prospectors. Being within two days' journey of the Indian country, a profitable trade is carried on with the knights of the plains.

While in the *Pioneer* office I sometimes had Indian callers, who would loiter about and smoke, as I performed the various duties of "getting out the paper." As they set a good example for civilized printing-office bores by not meddling with "copy," or confiscating "exchanges," they were tolerated.

Becoming weary of office confinement, I started .for the Yankton Sioux village. Here were Indians who had taken part in the Minnesota massacre, at New Ulm, in 1862, also at the previous carnage at Spirit Lake, on the line of Iowa and Minnesota, which occurred in 1856.

One day, while walking through the camp, I was astonished to find a little, blue-eyed girl, seven or eight years old, in a lodge with an Indian family. She was dressed and adorned like the Indian girls, and was happy and contented.

The sight of the little child among the savages. filled my mind with strange and varied conjectures.

Immediately I asked myself this question: "How did she come among them, and where are her parents?" A burning cabin, father and mother slain and the little orphan carried away into captivity, was the first scene to be imagined.

I addressed her in the Sioux tongue: "To-ken, chis-te-nah wah-se-cah wee?" (How do you do, little white woman?) She came to me immediately, and was glad to see one of her own race. Much of her early life had been forgotten, but she informed me that her name was Curry, that the Indians killed her mother and that her father and sister lived in the Brule camp.

While I was with the Yanktons a pony was sacrificed by a squaw. I had heard her mourning on the bluffs one night, as I lay on a bed of robes in an Indian lodge, and the next morning I joined a group of Indians who were standing around the dying pony. Her husband had died, and in order that his spirit might be joined, as she thought, on its journey to the "happy hunting-ground" by that of the pony, she sacrificed it by plunging a knife into its side, from which wound it bled to death.

One day while seated in company with an Indian family, with a heavy pipe-stem in my hand, I very thoughtlessly struck what I supposed to be a roll of furs, when to my surprise and mortification, a scream came from the bundle. A squaw at once sprang forward, unwrapped the package and took up a pretty, squalling, kicking, young pappoose, which the roll of furs proved to contain.

I endeavored to pacify the mother by explaining to her that I knew nothing of the baby being in the bundle, but she seemed to doubt it, and eyed me angrily. The father, however, looked upon the affair as the pardonable mistake it was, and so said nothing about it.

While watching two squaws painting the inside of a robe, an Indian who had just returned from a hunt, and who had not previously been aware of my presence in the camp, upon seeing me, raised his rifle and pointed it at me. Acting upon the impulse of the moment, I drew my revolver and presented it toward him, when he lowered his gun and approached me in a friendly manner.

After shaking my hand firmly, he proposed that we should practise with the revolver, which we did, but he would give me no explanation for his conduct upon first seeing me.

CHAPTER XII.

Far in the dark old forest glades,
　Where kalmias bloom around,
They had their place of youthful sport,
　Their childhood's hunting-ground;
And swinging lightly in the vines
　That o'er the wigwam hung,
The golden robins, building near,
　About their dwelling sung.

J. T. FIELDS.

THE SUPPOSED ORIGIN OF THE INDIANS—THEIR APPEARANCE AND DISPOSITION—DESIRE TO TORTURE—THE LIFE OF THE SQUAWS—WHAT THEY MUST DO—INDIAN MODE OF BURIAL.—MEDICINE MEN—THE STEAM BATH—INDIAN COURTSHIP AND MARRIAGE—"HOW MANY PONIES IS SHE WORTH?"—NAMES OF CHILDREN—LANGUAGE—THE REASON THE INDIANS HAVE NO BEARD—RAISING DOGS FOR FOOD—SUPERSTITIONS—WAR IMPLEMENTS—GAMES—DRYING MEAT—RELIGION—A CAMP—THE CONTENTS OF A WIGWAM—THE INDIAN WHO DESIRED THREE DAYS' RATIONS FOR ONE MEAL—HOW THEY COOK AND EAT—AN INDIAN MOTHER'S "HUSH-A-BY-BABY" SONG—TREATMENT OF INFANTS—SECRET SOCIETIES.

DURING my travels among the Indians I had an opportunity to observe their customs and mode of life, and I trust a chapter devoted to this subject will interest the reader.

The Indians seem to know very little about their origin, and the accounts they give are widely conflicting. The most substantial theory advanced by them, is, that at a very remote age, their ancestors emigrated to this country from another continent, and made the voyage in canoes, through a narrow neck of water. Perhaps they came from Asia, by way of Behring's Strait.

As a race, the North American Indians are tall, muscular and well formed. Having a dark copper color, high cheek-bones, long, black hair, flashing, restless, black eyes, their personal appearance, in general, is fierce and intimidating.

Their demeanor toward strangers is sullen and reserved. They regard every movement with suspicion, and are ever uneasy and watchful when in the presence of people whom they do not know or understand. When talking they are slow, cautious and weigh well the words they utter.

They are shrewd and cunning in many respects, still, owing to their disadvantages, they are most outrageously swindled by some of the whites. It has been said that they are devoid of the finer sentiments of mankind, but this, to a great extent, is an error. Hospitality, sociability and love for the beauty of Nature, are some of the redeeming traits in the character of these people.

They are taught from infancy that the white man is their enemy, and to fear and despise him, is one of the first lessons an Indian child receives from its parents, hence their cruelty toward their white foes. But is it any wonder that such feelings find a dwelling place within the savage breast?

A desire to torture is exhibited by the young at an early age. They delight in burning and mutilating any little animal that falls into their power. I once saw several Yankton Sioux boys standing around a pole, to which they had fastened a bird by means of a thorn piercing its body. First one of them would pull out a wing, then another a leg, or some feathers, at the same time laughing and shouting with delight.

No woman can have more than one husband, but a man can have as many wives as he can support. The wife does the more domestic labors, such as cutting wood, carrying water, erecting lodges, etc., while the husband performs the most fatiguing and difficult duty of scouring the prairies, climbing the mountain sides and fording the rivers, in quest of game for the wife and little ones.

The idea that the squaws must do all the work, while their liege lords do nothing but bask in the sunshine and smoke their pipes, originated in the imagination of the novelist. It is true the squaws work hard, but they don't do all that is done, nor the half of it. The Indian wife is generally contented, and if she knew as much about the average civilized husband as some of her white sisters do, it is not probable that she would exchange places with them.

Among different tribes, different modes of disposing of the dead prevail. The Sioux usually put the body upon an elevated platform, or among the branches of high trees. The platform or scaffold, is from six to ten feet high, and is made by driving four forked posts into the ground, poles next being laid across the top of the posts, and secured in the crotch with raw-hide thongs; other poles are then thrown across. Upon this frame the body is put, wrapped in a blanket or buffalo robe, and securely fastened with strips of buckskin.

All the personal property of the deceased, such as robes, ornaments, weapons and cooking utensils, are deposited with the body. In some cases, even the favorite horse and dog are led under the platform and shot, or strangled to death, in order, as the Indians believe, that their spirits may join their master's in "the land of cloudless skies."

There are always a number of these corpse receptacles near every stationary village, though they may be seen almost any place on the plains, in the Sioux country, and always upon a bluff, or elevated spot of ground.

There is something singularly impressive in the appearance of a Sioux cemetery. Nothing disturbs the solemn calm that reigns, save the sharp yelp of the hungry wolf, or the flight of shrieking vultures, as their freedom in the dreary solitude is disturbed by the tread of some venturesome traveler whose curiosity leads him to the spot, or by the approach of some Indian desiring to place upon the body of a departed friend, a few trinkets, or some food and water, which he imagines the spirit will come for.

The Chippewas and some of the Poncas place the body in a grave, in a sitting posture, with the face toward the East. The grave is not filled up, but a shed made of limbs and bark is erected over it. Thus the body can be seen at any time, and as the Indians generally embalm their dead, putrefaction does not take place.

Bun

On the death of an Indian, the lamentations of the friends are fearfully wild and distressing; they cut off their hair, blacken their faces, torture their bodies and give vent to their grief in franticness.

Among all tribes there is a class of individuals known as "medicine men," to whom the Indians resort in time of sickness. Although they make use of herbs, they have more faith in their horrid incantations. These doctors are very superstitious, and have an awe-inspiring power over the Indians.

While in Spotted Tail's camp, I often lay awake for hours at night, kept from sleep by the hideous groans and howls of some "medicine man," who was in a neighboring lodge endeavoring to drive off the evil spirit which he supposed sickened his patient. An old Sioux doctor showed me two tiny, round stones which he said enabled him to check diseases. I, of course, did not dare to dispute the truth of his assertion. He informed me that he had found the stones in the Black Hills.

They have certain times for making medicines, and conceal from each other a knowledge of the process. It is generally made in a lodge kept for the purpose, and is called by the Sioux, "pe-ju-tah te-pee," (medicine lodge). The contents of these lodges, or their appearance inside, I know nothing at all about, for I was never even allowed to peep into one of them. At nearly every lodge-door in a village, there are medicine-bags, containing herbs, fastened to a pole.

They have great faith in the steam-bath, which is procured in the following manner: First a tent, oval-shaped at the top, is made of poles securely covered with hides and blankets. Heated stones are then carried into the tent, and cold water poured upon them. As the lodge becomes well filled with steam thus formed, the patient is introduced in a nude condition.

When a young brave goes courting, he paints his face, dons his best breech cloth and moccasins, and drawing his blanket over his head and face, leaving an opening only large enough to see through, proceeds to meet his lady-love. Generally there is not as much love in Indian courtships as there is room for. and more wives are bought than won.

A young man seeing a maiden whom he thinks would make a good, patient, uncomplaining wife, at once proceeds to flatter her, makes her some presents, and then learns from her parents or friends how many ponies she is worth. Then, too, society among the savages is infested with the "scheming mamma" the same as it is in civilization, and she is ever looking for the "splendid chance."

Indians usually receive their names from objects surrounding them. They are Nature's offspring, and from it every want is supplied. The forests, mountains, plains, lakes and rivers, are their only text-books, and in them they are well versed.

Although a child receives a name at its birth, it is liable, in after years, to receive another, as events may occur in its lifetime that, according to Indian ideas, may suggest a new one.

Notwithstanding the great resemblance of one tribe to another, in general character, habits and personal appearance, and their intercourse by war, captivity and marriage, there is as much difference in the language of the various tribes as there is in that of the English, French or German.

The fact that the Indians have no beards is easily accounted for, as they pluck out every vestage of hair as fast as it appears on their face, commencing in boyhood. They have small tweezers made of wire, which they buy from the traders, and every time they dress and paint, they examine their faces carefully, and pull out any sign of a beard which they find. The eye-brows are likewise extirpated.

Among most tribes the dog is considered to be a sacred animal, and a feast of dogs' meat is always

an important accompaniment of a council or dance.
The Sioux devote much time and attention to raising dogs for food. They are great pets, and have
the freedom of the lodge. Often have I been kept
awake at night by the Indian dogs, who were either
fighting and snarling about the meat in the lodge,
or searching among the cooking utensils for food,
while my dusky companions were in "the land of
dreams," ignorant of the canine commotion.

Superstition has full sway among these people,
and, in consequence, they suffer needlessly. They
believe it necessary to solicit the extremes of heat
and cold, to fast for days at a time, and to cut and
injure their bodies. They think that the spirits of
their departed enemies return to earth to torture
them. To touch the fire with a knife, or to walk
between the fire and a person smoking a pipe, is an
omen of evil to come.

The bow and arrows have not been cast aside,
but are still quite popular, more because they are
Indian weapons than because the rifle would not
supply their place. To a great extent, stone implements of war and domestic use are things of the
past. However, the old stone war-clubs are still
to be found occasionally among some tribes, but in
most cases, they were made years ago by the more
primitive Indians, and are now retained by their
descendants as precious relics of the days when
there were few white people on Indian ground.

Stones somewhat shaped like an egg, and having one end flattened, which was occasioned by contact with a hard surface, and containing a light groove around the middle of them, have often been found by collectors of Indian relics. Speculations regarding their use were entertained.

While in Spotted Tail's camp, in 1878, I saw a few of these stones in use. They served the combined purpose of war-club, corn and meat pounder, and plum masher. A hammer was made of them in the following manner: A piece of green wood, about two and a half feet long, and half an inch thick, had been bent double over the stone, and being fitted into the groove, was there secured by tying the laps together. The whole frame, excepting the thick end of the stone, was then covered with raw-hide.

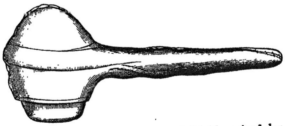

These implements are rare, and highly prized by

the Indians, but after some persuasion, and by pay-
ing a high price, I obtained one from each of the
Sioux warriors Cherry Stone and High Shield.

The engravings on the preceding page represent
the stone alone, and after it is covered and made to
do service as an implement of war and home use.

One of the Sioux sports is called the "tah-pah"
(ball) game. It is very much like what is known as
"shinny" by school-boys. There are always two
contesting parties, and the victorious one secures
the pledges, which generally consist of blankets,
robes, weapons or trinkets. The women engage in
the game with as much zeal as the men do. In the
summer evenings, after the duties of the day are
over, the squaws gather in groups, each one armed
with a stick about eighteen inches long, and curved
at one end, and from sun down till dark, they make
the village ring with their shouts of laughter and
mirth, as they pursue the bounding ball.

When more meat is obtained than is needed at
the time, the squaws cut it into thin strips and put
it upon poles, after which it is dried in the sun and
air. Although much meat is preserved in this way
during the summer, it is generally pure and sweet.
This is probably owing to the dry atmosphere of
the Western prairies.

Very few religious rites are performed by these
people, but they all believe in the existence of two
invisible, ruling spirits, the one good and kind, the

other evil, unkind and ever annoying them. They recognize fair weather, an abundance of game, etc., the gift of the Great Spirit.

After attacking a settlement, dwelling or wagon-train, the men, if any survive the assault, are shot, or tortured to death, and the women and children, should the Indians conclude to spare them, are retained as captives.

The camp-ground is usually selected in a grove, near a stream of running water, or a spring, but when on the prairies, these desirable features must be dispensed with to some extent. Some of these camps are quite extensive, often containing from five hundred to a thousand lodges, and averaging about five people to a lodge.

In the evening, during the summer months, an Indian village presents an interesting scene in the life of these people. Some of the women, old and young, are passing to and fro with loads of wood, meat, water and cooking-utensils; brawny warriors sit about in groups in the open air, smoking their pipes, mending weapons or recounting adventures; half naked and entirely nude children caper about in joyous freedom; young braves and dusky maids take their starlight-rambles; even the ponies and dogs form part of the scene as they stroll through the camp with perfect liberty.

A lodge is made in the following manner: From twelve to twenty yellow pine poles, about twenty feet in length, and stripped of the bark, are firmly tied together at the thin end, and after being put into an upright position, are carefully spread apart at the base, in order to form a staunch frame. A covering of raw-hide is then placed over it.

An opening is left at the top, where the ends of the poles meet, to let the smoke pass out. The lodge is entered by a small opening which serves as a door, but it is so small that a person must enter in a stooping position. A light, wooden frame which is covered with a piece of raw-hide, is used as a shutter, or door.

The contents of an ordinary lodge are composed of this list: Half a dozen Indians of various sizes, a number of dogs, some blankets and robes, bags made of ornamented raw-hide, clothing, weapons, cooking utensils, the pony's harness, wood, water, food and various other things. Full, crowded and packed, as it may seem to the reader, there is still room in the lodge for visitors, a fire in the center, and implements not in general use. The available part of a lodge is circular in form, and embraces a space of about ten feet in diameter.

During wet, stormy days, when there was little going on outside, I passed some pleasant hours in their cozy little tents. On such occasions the Indians, both old and young, would gather about me and request me to teach them, and tell them about the whites and their mode of life.

They often kept up the lodge-fire till midnight, or so long as I would remain awake and talk. In turn, they would sing for me, or relate their deeds in war and on the hunt.

I used to tell the Sioux that I intended to make a "wo-wah-pe" (book) for the white people to read, and that in it I would describe the Indian mode of life, and inform my people just how I fared at the hands of the Indians. This always pleased them, and doubtless influenced them to treat me well.

In the ravines, and along the rivers and creeks, in the Western Territories, wild fruit, berries and vegetables abound. Plums, cherries, grapes, currants, strawberries, raspberries and huckleberries, reach a high state of perfection, and are delicious. The squaws gather and dry large quantities for the winter months.

Wild potatoes, onions, turnips, artichokes and peas, are also found. The peas, however, would hardly be considered as being entitled to the name, in the East, on account of their non resemblance to domestic peas; but the Sioux name is "om-ah-ne-cha," which means peas, therefore I so term them. They grow on low, bushy stalks, the leaves of which somewhat resemble those of the parsnip. In appearance they look like small, green tomatoes, but taste like asparagus.

The Indians have no regular time for eating. If food is scarce, or if there is none to be had, they

will fast all of one day, and eat a dozen times the
next. I have often been astonished to see how an
Indian could dispose of quantities of half-cooked
meat at any hour of the day or night, yet dyspepsia
and other complaints of the stomach are rare.

A Sioux having been promised food enough for
three days, in pay for some service he did one of
the officers at Fort Randall, said:

"Let me have it all for dinner. I don't want to
be bothered by carrying it in my hands."

Meat is generally roasted or broiled: sometimes
it is boiled or stewed. Large pieces containing a
great deal of bone, are propped up against the fire
and left to roast by degrees. Small pieces are put
on a sharpened stake and held over the fire, when
they desire to roast or broil it, but when it is to be
boiled or stewed, they place it in a pot and suspend
it over the fire. All meat is cooked rare, and often
they prefer it entirely raw.

The Sioux squaws used to chant a song that always appeared strangely melancholy and affecting,
and seemed so much like a solemn dirge, that I
hesitated about inquiring the nature of it. When
I did so, I was greatly surprised upon being told
that the women were singing their babies to sleep.

I afterward observed that these gloomy strains
as effectually sent the little pappoose to "the land
of dreams," as the "hush-a-by-baby" of the white
mother puts her child to sleep.

An Indian mother loves her baby as much as any other mother loves hers, and she treats it just as tenderly in her own way. It gets no corn starch, farina or other delicacies, neither is it ever choked with paregoric, squills or soothing-syrup. While it is debarred from all these articles so well known to the majority of white infants, it can eat more half cooked meat, sleep longer and cry harder, than its baby brothers and sisters in civilization.

The pappoose is furnished a limited wardrobe at birth, and when the child becomes old enough to run alone, it is deprived of every vestige of dress during warm weather, until it reaches its fifth year. This is done in order to impart a rugged constitution, and to give room for the full development of the muscles and limbs.

The pappoose is carried in a small, tight-fitting receptacle made of raw hide or twigs, which rests on the mother's back, and is held in place with a buckskin strap supported by her forehead.

The Indian women are tolerably good cooks, the limited material and resources being duly noted. But very little can be said in their favor regarding cleanliness in their culinary affairs. The hampered way in which a family lives in a small tent, makes tidiness a secondary consideration.

Among the Sioux there is a secret and beneficial society. They have laws and rules that must be obeyed as promptly as those of the Odd Fellows,

Masons or Knights of Pythias. The meetings are opened with "a talk," then follow a dance and the other business of the meeting. The object of the order is help for the needy members.

The Indians are human nature in a savage, uncultured state, and, as such, on account of their manifold disadvantages and prejudice, are, as a people, cruel, treacherous and revengeful toward the white race. But they have always been so outrageously swindled by the whites, that much of their conduct can be overlooked.

Among Indians, as among all other people, no matter how harsh and relentless, there are many truly noble, sympathetic, generous natures. Then with charity—the natural outgrowth of our many advantages in a civilized and Christian land—let us overlook their failings, remembering that we are all the children of the one Great Spirit.

CHAPTER XIII.

Take me home to the place where I first saw light,
   To the sweet "Sunny South," take me home,
Where the mocking-bird sung me to sleep every night,
   Ah! why was I tempted to roam.

Take me home to the place where magnolias grow,
   To my cot in the evergreen shade,
Where the flowers on the river's green margin may blow
   Their sweets on the bank where we played.

                                          ANON.

BOUND FOR TEXAS—LIFE AMONG THE PENNSYLVANIA GERMAN
   FARMERS—ALEXANDRIA, MANASSAS AND LYNCHBURG—THE
   COLORED PEOPLE—BOTH SIDES OF SLAVERY—"DON'T AX
   WAR HE GOT DEM CHICKENS"—BRISTOL—JONESBOROUGH—
   KNOXVILLE—THE CONTRAST BETWEEN THE NORTHERN AND
   SOUTHERN PEOPLE—THE LADIES—A PRINTER'S INSTINCT—
   CHATTANOOGA AND ITS SURROUNDINGS—A PERILOUS RIDE
   ON A LOCOMOTIVE—MEMPHIS, LITTLE ROCK, TEXARKANA,
   DALLAS—A MODERN SODOM—HOW "THE POOR EDITOR" IS
   INTIMIDATED AT THE POINT OF A REVOLVER IN TEXAS—
   THE CLIMATE—THE COTTON FIELDS—NATURAL FEATURES.

ON leaving the Yanktons, I returned to Pennsylvania, where I remained till January, 1878, and
then started for Texas, by way of York, Baltimore,
Washington, Lynchburg, Knoxville, Chattanooga,
Memphis and Little Rock.

York, Pennsylvania, an old and wealthy interior
city, is located on Codorus Creek, eighty-nine miles
from Philadelphia, and fifty-nine from Baltimore.

It is engaged in the manufacture of railroad cars and farming implements, and is the county seat of York County, a fine agricultural district.

The farmers of this county, like those of Lancaster, Lebanon, Berks, Lehigh and other eastern counties of Pennsylvania, are known far and wide as the "Pennsylvania Germans," an upright, sturdy class of people, who are noted for their generosity and hospitality to both friends and strangers. .

They are plain and unassuming in their manners, remarkably destitute of suspicion, hate, hypocrisy and pride, and are not encumbered by the useless forms and styles of city people. When friends or strangers happen to meet them while at meals, or about meal-time, they present no lavish or stereotyped form of invitation. They will say:

"Doo, belibsht doch, zum mit-dag esse," (you, of course, will stay for dinner,) or, "Kum setz dich by, un nems mit uns wes mere hen"(come sit up, and accept what we have). They seldom help company, but say:

"Yets, helf dich selver" (now, help yourself).

Just before the Battle of Gettysburg, during the Rebellion, a straggling party of our friends from the Southern Land visited York County, and some of them, we believe, expressed themselves thus:

"Well, boys, we have reached 'the land of milk and honey.' Here wheat bread, apple-pies and beef, grow upon every fence-rail. Let each try to find a wife among these Dutch girls, stop right here, and leave 'Dixie' do her own fighting on a corn-bread and bacon diet."

The language these people speak is a dialect of the South German, and is simple, less involved, and requires fewer words to express an idea than other German dialects.

The first attempt at literature in the Pennsylvania German language was by Dr. Harbaugh, author of *'S Alt Schul-haus an der Krick*, (The Old School-house on the Creek,) and other poems, which, after his death, were issued under the title of *Harbaugh's Harfe*, (Harbaugh's Harp). The poetic merit of the work gained for it great popularity and a wide circulation.

In 1879 another book of poems in the same dialect, under the title of *'S Alt Marik-haus Mittes in der Schtadt, un de Alte Zeite*, (The Old Market-house in the Middle of the Town, and the Olden Times,) was written and published by H. L. Fisher, a well-known lawyer of York, Pennsylvania, and a relative of the deceased Dr. Harbaugh.

This latter work is in two principal parts, contains nearly three hundred pages and is illustrated with over one hundred engravings. The whole is a poetic production of literary merit, pathos and original humor. It goes right home to the heart of the reader who appreciates home-life among the Pennsylvania German farmers, and who loves these mild, quiet, kind-hearted people. The work is one grand, vivid, interesting panorama-like view of farm life among the Pennsylvania Germans of several generations ago, as well as of the present time.

On reaching Baltimore, Washington and Alexandria, the traveler from the North finds that much of the Southern element and custom exists among the people. Even in Baltimore this is more noticeable than might be supposed, more so than it is in Washington, for in the latter city are found people from every state and territory in the Union, as well as from all parts of the civilized world.

A heavy snow fell while I was in Washington, and extended as far south as East Tennessee, and in the mountains between Lynchburg and Bristol, it was deeper than it had been for years before.

Alexandria, on the Potomac River, seven miles below Washington, is a city of about sixteen thousand people. The river here forms a good harbor, and considerable light shipping is carried on. The aspect of the city, and the manners and customs of the people, are emphatically Southern, and at once after leaving the Potomac and proceeding south, the traveler cannot fail to see that he has departed from "Yankeedom" and is entering "Dixie." But he will meet as good people as he left behind.

Manassas, twenty-eight miles from Alexandria, is a small village that has gained a place in history on account of having been in close proximity to the formidable Battles of Manassas, fought during the late Civil War. The stranger passing through this quiet little town is surprised and pained on hearing its citizens recall the scenes of bloodshed and strife that once destroyed its peacefulness.

Lynchburg is situated on a bluff overlooking the James River and some of the most picturesque uplands in "Old Virginia." It is surrounded by an extensive tobacco-raising country, and is the center of the Virginia tobacco trade.

My travels led me into every Southern State, and into all the principal Southern cities and towns, but I never saw a more complete representation of the colored element, as it appears in the streets on Saturday afternoon, than I did in Lynchburg.

Although the snow was a foot in depth, which is not usual in this place, hundreds of colored folks, of both sexes, and of almost every size and age to be found, were loitering about the streets. Women and children were either eying the contents of the store-windows, watching the finely-dressed ladies or chatting with their friends, while the men were tampering with politics, watching for an opportunity to "tote dat package right down to de ke-ars," or urging through the streets, stubborn oxen drawing two-wheeled carts containing "de colla'd ladies and gemmen from de country."

No matter how poor, ragged or abused they may be, they are ever happy and cheerful among them-

selves, and polite and obliging to " dem stucked up
white folks."

Although some of the former slaves were abused,
oppressed and regarded as being no better than animals, by some ignorant, cruel, small-souled masters,
their cheerful temperament doubtless proved to be
a comfort in the midst of their hardships.

There were some heartless masters who worked
their slaves from four o'clock in the morning till ten
o'clock at night, whipped them shamefully and did
not give them even enough fat bacon and corn-meal
to eat; but it must be remembered that this was the
exception, and not the general rule.

I would not have the reader understand me as asserting that all the slaves were harshly dealt with,
or that the Southerners are harsh, cold-hearted and
cruel, for such is as far from being a fact as that the
beautiful orange-groves and cotton-fields could be
successfully transplanted on the snow-clad summits
of the Alleghany Mountains.

About the first words a traveler hears as the cars
stop at a station in the South, are these : "Here's
yer nice, tender chicken, hot coffee and waffles!" and
the next moment, good-natured old Sambo or Aunt
Hannah comes to the car-window, carrying on his
or her head a large waiter containing nicely fried
chicken and waffles, as well as a shining coffee-pot
full of steaming Java.

A too inquisitive Yankee traveler once asked " old

uncle" where he "raised" the chickens he was then selling, and the reply was in words about like these:

"Look he-ah boss, I reckon you's from de Norf, and if dat am de case, you, to be course, is a friend ob de black race. So please don't ax dis chile war he got de chickens."

Bristol, Tennessee, through which the west line of Virginia passes, is a village of about thirty-five hundred inhabitants, and is surrounded by a mountainous region. It is noted as a rendezvous for the runaway lovers of Virginia. As marriages between minors are not valid in Virginia, Bristol is a place of shelter for the matrimonially-inclined rising generation of the "Old Dominion State." Here they can readily obtain license, secure the services of a minister and thus defy the wrath of an angry father and a troublesome mother-in-law.

Jonesborough, thirty-two miles from Bristol, on the railroad leading on to Knoxville, contains about fifteen hundred people, but it is one of the oldest towns in Tennessee. It is surrounded by a good limestone farming country, which only requires the industry of a Northern element to make it what it was before the ravages of war blighted its surface.

Jonesborough is the seat of *Martin Academy*, an institution of learning for both sexes, where the primary branches, as well as Greek, Latin, French, &c., are taught. The academy is under the management of the Rev. W. G. Barker, a Southern gentleman of wide experience as an educator, and possessed of frank, genial manners.

Knoxville, on the Holston, or Tennessee River, is an attractive little city of about twelve thousand inhabitants. It is handsomely located on bluffs, and commands a fine view of the surrounding country. During high water, steamboats ascend the river to this point from Chattanooga. It was laid out in 1794, and was once the seat of State Government.

A great difference exists between the people of the North and the South, in manners, customs and general way of thinking and doing. Northern people are better educated, quicker in thought and act, more energetic and persevering, and brighter and smarter in their general make up, than their friends in the South; but they are far from being as kind, sociable, generous and hospitable, as the people of the South are.

If you ask a Northern man the distance to a place, he will "take you in" with one sweeping glance of his calculating eyes, and, answering your question in an instant, is gone. But ask a Southern man the same question and he will be three times as long in answering it, but he will do it in such a kind, frank and interested manner, that the time he consumes is not regretted.

Should you make a similar inquiry of a Southern countryman, his answer would probably be this:

"Wall, stranger, it's right smart of a distance. I

reckon it's nigh on ten miles, and it's a sorter bad road, too. What might your name be?"

A contrast between the Northern and Southern ladies is very noticeable. Northern ladies are more forward, self-reliant and business-like, than most of their Southern sisters are. But the Southern lady is handsomer, kinder and gentler.

A Northern lady can make a shirt, mend trowsers and wash and dress her own baby, but a Southern lady usually turns this duty over to a black servant.

Very little yeast bread is used in the South, but warm biscuits are a three-times-a-day luxury. They are usually baked in a Dutch oven, in the fire-place, as the abundance of wood in the South naturally prompts the people to dispense with coal-stoves, and cling to the cheerful, old-fashioned fire-hearth.

In the mansion of the rich man, as well as in the negro hut, sweet potatoes, hominy, corn-bread and bacon, form a favorite meal. Southern ladies know how to spread their tables with good things, and they have the articles in their pantries to do it with, but there seems to be some merit in fat pork and corn-bread that induces them to give it prominence.

As I trust that my little book will find its way in to many homes in the beautiful Southern land, I hope that none of my lady readers will be offended at thus having their culinary affairs tampered with by a meddlesome "Yankee," for I love the South and its people—all the ladies included.

One day I was hailed by a young man who said: "Say, stranger, are you a printer? I always think I can recognize a brother typographer as far off as I can see him."

Between Lynchburg and Chattanooga the country is mountainous, but the soil is more productive than that of the level and pine-timbered sections of the Southern States. Fine forests of oak, chestnut and hickory abound, also noble springs and streams.

Chattanooga, on the Tennessee River, is a growing city, and a railroad center of importance. It is largely engaged in manufacturing iron, and is called "the Pittsburgh of the South." The city is environed by lofty, timbered mountains, the highest of which is the Lookout Mountain. Chattanooga was the scene of some terrible battles fought during the Rebellion. A great many Northern people have located here since the war.

After working awhile on newspapers in Chattanooga, and in Huntsville, Alabama, I proceeded to Memphis, thence on to Texas.

Leaving Huntsville one night, I rode to Tuscumbia on a locomotive with the engineer, and I shall never forget the ride. It was a night run, and we were behind time, but the engineer wanted to pass the reverse-bound train at the usual point.

About two o'clock in the morning we started from a little town five miles distant from the place where the trains were accustomed to pass each other. We were so late that the engineer of the other train would naturally think that we were greatly behind time, and suppose that instead of trying to pass at the usual place, we would lay over at some other point beyond him.

A collision, therefore, somewhere on the five miles of track, was very apt to occur. A grade was just ahead, which was very disadvantageous to us, but the engineer pulled the throttle-valve open, and the fireman shoveled coal into the roaring furnace until the perspiration rolled in great drops from his face.

The conductor came over the top of the train to the locomotive and asked the engineer what he was doing and where he was going. "To meet the train five miles from here!" was the answer. In vain the conductor urged him to go back, and not run the risk of meeting the other train half-way, he put on every available pound of steam, and watched the track ahead.

As the ponderous machine thundered over the rails at the rate of a mile a minute, many thoughts crowded through my mind, while in almost breathless suspense I gazed in front for the head-light of the locomotive which I expected would dash into us every time we rounded a curve.

After we left the grade, the momentum and rocking of the locomotive was fearful. I looked for it to leave the track, or crush into the other train at any second.

At such a time—when death stares us in the face, man's weakness and insignificance comes vividly to mind, and we eagerly turn to Him, whom, in our daily walks of life, we are so prone to forget.

My own face, of course, I could not see, but the conductor's was the wildest and most distressed I ever saw. Even the engineer became frightened at his own rashness. The few moments seemed like hours, but at last we whirled around the curve that hid the side-track from view, and saw the head-light of the other train just as it was leaving the switch.

Instantly both engineers shut off steam, but the locomotives could only be stopped within a few feet of each other. A sigh of relief burst from each of us when the engine ceased to move, and all realized that a horrible death had been escaped.

Memphis, situated on the Mississippi River, at the head of perpetual steamboat navigation, is the largest Southern commercial center north of New Orleans. Prior to the war, the people of Memphis were very wealthy, but many of them have since experienced a reverse of fortune.

From this point I went to Little Rock, Arkansas, a handsome little city finely located on the Arkansas River. An air of comfort and neatness pleasing to a stranger, surround the homes of this capital city.

Passing through the swamps and pine forests of Southwestern Arkansas, I entered the "Lone Star State" at Texarkana. Here I found a border town full of life and energy, as well as saloons and faro-banks. From here I proceeded to Marshall, thence to Tyler, where I worked awhile on the *Courier*, and then went to Dallas, Sherman and Denison.

Of all the cities I ever visited, North or South, East or West, Dallas, considering its size, contains more business energy, more fast men and women, less morality, more day and night card playing and more unmasked wickedness, than any of them.

Dallas differs from all the other Southern cities in point of morality and refinement. Its population consists of people from almost every country in the world, and the elements of the genuine Southern city are not to be found in this modern Sodom.

At McKinney I stopped a few days with T. E. Bomar, editor of the *Advocate*, and assisted him to get out an issue of his paper. He related to me the following circumstance, which occurred in his experience as an editor while publishing a paper in Sherman, during the late war, when revolvers and bowie-knives were in daily use in Texas:

He published an item that was true and proper, concerning one of the city desperados, which so enraged the individual, that he went to the office of publication armed with a six-shooter. Going up to Mr. Bomar, he commenced the following dialogue:

"Is the editor in?"

"Yes sir!"

"Are you the man?"

"I am!"

"Did you write that item about me?"

"Yes sir!"

"Well sir, (drawing his pistol) it's a falsehood!"

"Yes!"

"Of course, you will take it all back!"

"Certainly, sir, certainly!"

The victorious intimidator then left the office, as a sigh of relief burst from the horror-stricken quill-driver, who realized that he had narrowly escaped an editor's possible fate.

When the Northern States are snow-bound, the climate in Texas is warm and delightful. In most parts of the state winter is unknown, and the grass and flowers are ever present. The change from Pennsylvania's rigid clime to this land of sunshine and flowers, was truly enchanting.

At a distance, the vast fields of cotton, when in bloom, resemble great tracts of snow. Cotton is one of the principal crops of the state.

The eastern part of the state, from the west line of Louisiana to the Trinity River, consists largely of immense pine forests, under-brush and swamps. The western section is one vast tract of undulating prairie land. In the extreme northwest the surface becomes mountainous, and in the southwest is El Llano Estacado or Staked Plain, a table-land destitute of water, grass or timber. Buffaloes, wild-horses and antelope, still roam the prairies.

CHAPTER XIV.

Along the winding Ponca
  Stretch the wigwams of the Sioux.
Half hid in grass and flowers,
  And o'erhung by skies of blue.

A. H. G.

I LEAVE TEXAS FOR DAKOTA—CAMPING—A NARROW ESCAPE—
THE INDIAN TERRITORY—LAWRENCE AND LEAVENWORTH—
JOSEPH, CHIEF OF THE NEZ PERCES—A ROMANTIC LADY—
ST. JOSEPH, COUNCIL BLUFFS, OMAHA, CHEYENNE, OGDEN,
SACRAMENTO, OAKLAND, SIOUX CITY—THE WINNEBAGOES—
I VISIT SPOTTED TAIL'S VILLAGE—CAMP SCENES—STANDING
ELK—A BREAKFAST—A FEATHER DANCE—SPOTTED EAGLE—
HOW A SIOUX TREATS HIS MOTHER-IN-LAW—HOW MY BEEF
DISAPPEARED—AN INDIAN'S ACCOUNT OF CUSTER'S BATTLE—
FINGER-BONES FOR A NECKLACE—INDIAN HOSPITALITY—I
AM OFFERED A SIOUX WIFE—A STORM—TAKING NOTES.

LEAVING Texas, I started to Dakota Territory.
One night, while passing through the Indian Territory, I camped out with two travelers about forty
miles north of the Red River. After cooking our
supper, we made a bed of limbs and prairie-grass,
and then built a fire, to keep off the wolves that
were prowling around.

One day, while walking along the Boggy River
in company with a Choctaw Indian, he suddenly
drew his revolver and fired at some animal in the
timber, near by. and came very near shooting me

instead. He was a few feet in advance of me when
he stopped to draw his revolver, and not noticing
what he was doing, I walked on, and was so close
to him when he fired, that the powder burned my
face, as I was on the side from which he fired.

At McAlister, Indian Territory, I worked awhile
on the *Star Vindicator*, a journal printed partly in
the English and partly in the Indian language. I
then resumed my journey northward.

The portion of the Indian Territory traversed
by the Missouri, Kansas & Texas Railway consists
of undulating prairie, which, as yet, is very thinly
settled by the whites. Railway stations are from
twenty to thirty miles apart, and generally consist
of nothing more than a frame depot and the few
buildings occupied by the railway employes.

Vinita, situated in the northeastern part of the
territory, and at the crossing of the Missouri, Kansas & Texas, and the St. Louis and San Francisco
Railways, is a small border town partly inhabited
by civilized Cherokee Indians. It will probably, in
the future, become a prominent trade-center.

Lawrence, on the Kansas River, is a beautiful
city, and contains about ten thousand people. It
figured prominently in the Kansas slavery troubles
of 1854, but upon its handsome streets and in its
happy, refined homes remain no trace of the strife
and bloodshed for which it was once noted.

Leavenworth, on the Missouri River, is the me-

tropolis of Kansas. Before the event of railroads
west of the Missouri, Leavenworth was one of the
principal outfitting points for overland emigrants.
The population is twenty-two thousand.

The population of cities and towns as found in
this work, is according to the local census of the
respective places up to 1879.

Two miles from the City of Leavenworth is Fort
Leavenworth, the finest and most handsomely situated military post in the West. Within late years
it has been used merely as a supply post for forts
further West.

Near this garrison I visited Chief Joseph and
his band of Nez Perces Indians, with whom the
whites had been at war the summer previous, but
who were now captives of the Government There
were four hundred in the party, all encamped in
the timber along the Missouri.

When I informed them that I had lived among
the Sioux, they became very friendly, and wanted
to know how many days' travel it was to the Sioux
country, as the greater part of the tribe had joined
Sitting Bull in Montana before Chief Joseph sur-
rendered to the military.

I was sociably entertained by Joseph, and given
a seat on his couch, where he was sitting when I
entered his lodge. He showed me some letters of
recommendation that had been given him by military men, before the intrusion of squatters upon

his reservation had forced him to go to war. He
also exhibited a gold ring, which a romantic white
lady had given him for the privilege of helping herself to a kiss.

He is a man of fine presence, but is modest and
unassuming. He talks but little, seems absorbed
in thought and is quiet and reserved. He is a man
whom an observer of human nature would, at once,
recognize as having more depth of mind than idle
prattle and boasting on the end of his tongue.

After leaving the Nez Perces, I proceeded on my
journey, going by the way of Atchison, St. Joseph,
Council Bluffs, Sioux City and Yankton. Atchison
and St. Joseph are fine, thriving towns, situated on
the Missouri.

Council Bluffs is located on the Missouri, opposite Omaha. It is bounded on the east by a ridge
of high, timbered bluffs. Lewis and Clark, who
ascended the Missouri to its source, in 1806, held a
council with the Indians on the site of the city, and
from that circumstance it received its name.

Omaha is situated on highlands, on the western
bank of the Missouri. It is the largest city in the
State of Nebraska, and is a great trading point for
a wide scope of farming country. It is the head-
quarters of the Union Pacific Railroad Company,
which is a great support to the city.

The principal cities on the line of the Union and
Central Pacific Railroads, which I visited while on

my trips to California, are Fremont, Grand Island, North Platte, Cheyenne, Ogden, Sacramento and Oakland.

The first three mentioned places are fine, growing towns, and are in the midst of excellent farm and stock raising districts.

Cheyenne, the capital of Wyoming, is one of the principal supply points for the Black Hills and the Big Horn and Yellow Stone Countries. In early days, it was the scene of many bloody encounters between the bordermen and hunters who formed the population of the place.

Ogden, Utah, a Mormon city, is situated between the Ogden and Weber Rivers. A stream of water flows on each side of the streets, which is a very attractive and pleasing feature. The buildings are small, but are enchantingly embowered in orchards and gardens.

Sacramento, the capital of California, is located on the Sacramento River. The houses are built of brick, and the streets are broad and well shaded by fine trees. Steamboats ply between this city and San Francisco. I remember with pleasure, a trip between the two cities on the steamer *New World*.

It is not an unusual sight to see the bearing fig-trees towering above the dwellings. The Chinese form a fair portion of the population, and make a good livelihood, still, many of them think that the "Mellican man no good, muchee rob poor Chinee."

Oakland is the terminus of the Pacific Railroad, and is situated on the eastern shore of the Bay of San Francisco, two miles from the metropolis, with which it is connected by a ferry. It is a handsome place, and is surrounded by delightful villas, vineyards and forests.

I beg the reader's pardon for this digression, and will now resume the account of my journey from Texas to Dakota.

Leaving Council Bluffs, I proceeded up to Sioux City. This is a pretty place, on the Missouri, five miles from the Dakota line.

About thirty miles below Sioux City, I visited a camp of Winnebago Indians. In various respects they resemble the Chippewas, and construct their lodges with bark and a species of water reed.

Reaching Yankton, Dakota, I continued on up to Niobrara, Nebraska. From this point I was sent to Spotted Tail's camp by a western journal. In the Sioux village I prepared several sketches on Indian camp life for the paper, and though copied by the *New York Herald* and other journals, I insert extracts from them in this chapter.

Writing has always been a pleasure to me, for I seem to be holding intercourse with dear, unseen friends, who receive my printed thoughts as a face to face conversation. With an author's pardonable whim, I love to fancy myself visiting the firesides where my modest little book is read, and to imagine the warm hearts and smiling faces I would find.

To all those friends whose forms I have never seen, and whose voices I have never heard, I send greeting, with kind wishes for happiness and pleasant paths.

Crossing the Missouri River to the Dakota side, I proceeded up the river to a point near Choteau Creek, where I crossed over again, landing near the mouth of Ponca River; then traveling along that stream until the Indian village was reached.

The camp consisted of nearly the entire Brule Sioux nation, and contained about eight hundred lodges and five thousand Indians. This immense village was scattered along the river for a distance of fifteen or more miles.

Entering the narrow, but beautiful valley of the Ponca, a scene ever grand and fascinating to me, lay before me. As far as the eye could reach, were the tall, white lodges, and groups of gaily dressed Indians; some hurrying to and fro, others sitting on the ground, in clusters, or galloping across the hills after stampeding ponies.

At first, upon entering the camp, the Sioux were rather rude, and regarded me with suspicion, but upon learning that I had lived among their people before, and understood their language, they became quite friendly.

Entering the lodge of Standing Bear, he greeted me cordially, and was very communicative. After some conversation, we took dinner, the meal consisting of meat and coffee, placed on a blanket, on the lodge floor—the naked ground.

As I proceeded up the valley, the lodges, as well as the Indians, became more numerous, while the bluffs, on both sides of the river, were strewn with hundreds of ponies grazing. .

The first night I stopped with Standing Elk, and was treated with kindness and attention. He informed me that, when he was a young man, his old father used to tell him to stop fighting the whites and be their friend. The military, however, know that he has not always followed this advice.

Some years ago, Spotted Tail and a band of his warriors robbed the Overland Mail Coach of the money it contained, and murdered the escort and passengers. He was captured by the soldiers, and taken to the East, accompanied by Standing Elk who succeeded in having him restored to his tribe.

He desired to know why I ventured to his camp, and was much pleased when I informed him that I had always taken an interest in his race, sympathized with them in their oppression by the whites, and would give a good account of them upon my return to civilization.

He had but one wife, and remarked, that when at Washington to see the President, he saw that white men had only one wife, and as he deemed it good policy, he concluded to follow their example.

When bedtime arrived, a comfortable couch was made for me by Mrs. Standing Elk, and I lay down to sleep, while the noise of the drums and whoops of the wild dancers in a neighboring lodge, rang upon the still night air.

As I lay there, surrounded on all sides by these strange, nomadic people in their primitive charac teristics, my thoughts reverted to my own singular situation. Though alone in the heart of the camp, at midnight, and at the mercy of the Indians, fear hardly entered my mind, for I was with the Sioux, a people who have always been more hostile and troublesome to the Government than any other In dians in the West, yet among whom I have seldom found aught but kindness and friendship, when I might readily have been killed and scalped.

Sometime during the night a storm arose, and considerable rain fell, but I slept comfortably and dry. In the morning. I wondered where the dry wood to make a fire with, was to come from, but Mrs. Standing Elk enlightened me by drawing a pile of dry brush from under her bed, with which she started a fire, afterward adding some wet wood from the outside.

For breakfast we had hot cakes, meat and coffee. The Indians are not very fond of bread, but having a little agency flour sometimes, they occasionally make bread, or a kind of short-cake. Meat alone, without salt or pepper, is a favorite article of food.

During the day I witnessed the feather dance, a ceremony which does not differ much from other dances common among the Sioux The drummers assembled in the dance lodge first, and commenced the strange, weird music of the ceremony. Then callers went about the village arousing the dancers.

Soon the tent, a very large one made by putting several ordinary sized ones together, was filled with the most hideously painted and adorned warriors it is possible to imagine, all sitting cross legged, in a circle Several large kettles containing the flesh of dogs, were placed in the middle of the lodge, for the feast A few of the Indians then arose up and began to dance to the music of the drums.

At intervals of fifteen or twenty minutes they would sit down to rest, and recount their exploits in war. Then they would arise again, and continue the dance, joined each time, by more Indians, until every brave in the lodge was leaping and whooping

The whole ceremony was wild and furious in the extreme, and presented a scene of mingled paint, feathers, bells, beads and half naked Indians, that baffles a just description. Their faces were daubed with red, yellow, blue and black paint, while their heads were adorned with feathers and porcupine quills, and their legs with bells and other trinkets.

Several squaws were seated directly behind the drummers, and, at intervals, sang the praise of the assembled braves, as is the custom at such dances.

In the course of an hour, one of the dancers took a cluster of feathers, which was secured to a belt, and fastened it upon his back. He then danced for about ten or more minutes, and afterward made a short speech.

One of the Indians then placed a piece of dogs' meat into the mouth of each of about half of the warriors assembled, and after flourishing another piece above his head, and uttering a few words in a low tone, he threw it into the fire as an offering to the Great Spirit. Each brave was then served with a dishful of the meat.

While the men were dancing, a number of squaws had a grand feast all to themselves, on the prairie, several hundred yards from the dance-lodge; but some who did not attend the feast, stood before the lodge watching the dancers.

The following night I witnessed another dance, but it was much wilder in its character than some others, and the Indians carried with them a number of their weapons and a few human scalps, which, in the dim light of the waving fire-brands, I supposed to be those of white women. The sight of these trophies of carnage filled my mind with awe and forebodings, but I revealed not my thoughts, nor asked questions concerning the scalps.

The speakers brandished their pistols, and spoke much about the wrongs inflicted upon them by the whites. Two little boys, gaily dressed and painted, also took part in the dance. They probably were the sons of a chief, and were being mustered into the rank of Sioux warriors.

It being customary to place food before a visitor, and a great breach of Indian politeness for him to refuse it, no matter how often he may have eaten during the day, I was astonished at my appetite.

One evening, while near Spotted Eagle's lodge, he very kindly invited me to pass the night in his wigwam. Although I informed himself and wives that I had already eaten supper, I noticed a change came over their dusky countenances, and so I tried to eat some of the meat that was placed before me.

Spotted Eagle had two wives, who were cousins, and they seemed to agree very well. One of them made a comfortable bed near the fire for me, and as the night was cold, Spotted Eagle covered me with his own blanket, in addition to the covering already furnished me.

In the morning we went visiting, and while in a neighboring lodge, an old squaw looked in, but left immediately. Spotted Eagle at the same moment covered his head with his blanket. It was one of his mothers-in-law, and as a Sioux warrior seldom speaks to his mother-in-law, or even looks at her, if he can avoid it, the unexpected meeting caused the strange conduct of both.

Such a state of affairs, although far from being right or agreeable, would be quite satisfactory to many married men in civilization, who are troubled by meddlesome mothers-in-law.

One day while I was in the village, some of the Indians shot a herd of cattle which they had driven from one of the settlements on the Missouri. A grand time was had at the slaughter, and the feasts that followed were characteristic of the gormandizing propensity of the Indians.

Going to where they were cutting up one of the animals, I found a group of men, women, children and dogs, gathered around the carcass, eating raw meat with an evident relish. The marrow, heart, liver and brains, seemed to be their choice of the beef. The children and squaws were hunting out the marrow while the bones were yet warm.

An old warrior, who was devouring the raw beef with the appetite of a ravenous wolf, invited me to join him, and when I declined, he laughed derisively at my white-womanish notion, while the women and children jeered the white man who could not eat uncooked meat.

When their merriment was over, they gave me a piece of steak which I had selected, and I then proceeded to a lodge, near by, where an Indian gave me a pan and some salt, when I fried the meat.

Taking a piece out of the pan to see if it needed to remain longer on the fire, I told the Indian to help himself, and he did so. After stirring the fire, I reached for the pan, when, to my surprise, I saw that it was about empty, and the Indian was smacking his lips and preparing for a smoke.

Seeing some young braves fishing in the Ponca River, which, by the way, is only a small creek, I concluded to join them, but their hooks were dull, and so I could catch no fish.

I then offered to shoot at a mark with the young men, which they readily agreed to. Soon a crowd collected, and many trials were made, White Turtle proving himself to be the best marksman.

After the trial was over, Brave Bull, the nimblest Indian, in both tongue and limbs, I ever saw, asked me to accompany him to his lodge. Here I met a warrior who had taken part in the Sioux resistance of Custer's attack upon their village. He had a number of finger-bones on a cord around his neck, wearing them both as an ornament, and as a trophy of his success in battle.

As General Custer and every man in his party fell in the battle with Sitting Bull, the accounts of the affair were very unreliable and contradictory, having been based alone upon supposition and the appearance of the battle-field after the Indians had left. The Western newspaper story to the effect that one of its reporters interviewed Sitting Bull soon after the fight, and was informed by him that Custer and his men stood on a little hill, and fell "like shocks of corn," one after another—Custer last—appears to be about as near the truth as some other newspaper "accounts" that originate in the brilliant minds of the enterprising, but not over-truthful sensational reporters.

The following account of the fight, though unlike any other I ever heard or read, was related to me by Indians who had left Sitting Bull shortly after the battle, and had joined Spotted Tail's tribe. I give it to the reader without hesitancy, as I deem it to be as reliable, or at least as plausible, as any of the accounts heretofore published:

The Sioux said that when General Custer attack-ed their camp, they were in a narrow valley through which flowed a stream, which from their description, must have been a branch of the Little Big Horn. Upon entering the valley, Custer suddenly found a small camp consisting of about one hundred tents, which he attacked furiously, and slaughtered men, women and children, like cattle, before the warriors had time to make any available resistance.

Some of the Indians who escaped, dashed off on horseback to the main village, where Sitting Bull and Crazy Horse were encamped with a large and well armed body of warriors, and informed them what was happening at the little outskirt-camp.

General Custer, being elated by his easily-won victory so far, probably supposed that he could successfully cope with any body of Indians that he might meet. He, however, as circumstances prove, knew not that a few miles distant, was the most

war-like band of warriors perhaps ever assembled
west of the Mississippi since Black Hawk's war.

On the arrival of this startling news, the Indians
hurriedly prepared for battle, and then, like a vast,
sweeping wave, pressed through the valley, bearing
down upon the doomed Custer and his command.
Maddened at the sight of their dead friends, the
Sioux rushed upon the troops with fearful yells and
war-hoops.

General Custer now, for the first time, must have
realized his grave error with a fainting heart, as his
men drooped and wavered before the overwhelming
host that surrounded them. Seeing that the Sioux
outnumbered him fifty to one, he hastily endeavored
to retreat, but the Indians actually rode in among
the soldiers, and with repeating rifles and revolvers,
carried on a carnage seldom equaled in warfare.

The troops became so intimidated and confused
at sight of the fearful odds that confronted them,
that they offered very little resistance after firing
the first volley.

The affair was over in thirty minutes, and instead
of Custer and his men falling close together on a
little hill, as some reports declared, the Indians said
that those who escaped the first onslaught, unconsciously retreated toward a high embankment over-
hanging the little stream, where they were pressed
to leap over into the rocky stream below, and those
who were not killed by the fall, the Indians shot.

One night the weather, though it was now about the middle of April, became quite cold and stormy, and when I retired, the Indians divided their bedding with me. A robe and two blankets were found for me to lie upon, the men then covered me with three blankets and asked if I was comfortable.

Sometime during the night I awoke, and by the dim light of the dying embers, I could discern the forms of my dusky companions who were now fast asleep, each person being covered with but a single blanket, or rather a part of one, for two slept under one blanket, while the rain and sleet beat upon the lodge furiously.

Here was an exhibition of Indian hospitality, and it effected me not a little to think that they would cover me—one of the much despised white race—with three blankets, while they had but half a one apiece, and that, too, on one of the coldest nights of the season. Surely, there is within the Indian breast, that fount of human kindness and affection, the existence of which, it is so popular to doubt.

Brave Bull desired me to teach him to read and write, in order, as he said, that the whites could not cheat him. With a lead-pencil I made the letters of the alphabet, and succeeded in teaching him to pronounce them, also to spell words of one syllable. He displayed an unusually good memory, and was very apt and eager to learn.

Medicine Lake wanted me to remain with him to

teach his family, saying that he and his wife would be a good father and mother to me.   He said:

"I will pay you with ponies, or any thing I have that you might want, and I will give you my best daughter for a wife, if you will remain here, be my son and teach our children."

The Indians desired to know what my profession was, and when I informed them that I was a printer —one who makes "speaking books and papers"— they were pleased, and requested me to remember them honestly in my new book.

Sometimes, while among the Sioux, I had papers with me containing articles on Indian life that I had written while on some previous visit to the tribe; these I would explain to the Sioux, who were eager listeners, and were amazed to learn, that what had transpired among their people a short time before, was chronicled upon the printed sheet before them.

One night a terrific storm raged, blowing down a number of tents, and the rain fell in torrents.   The lodge I slept in leaked considerably, and I awoke to find myself lying in a pool of water.   Toward day, the wind broke the lodge in several places, causing quite a commotion among the women and children, and all of us got a thorough drenching.

The Sioux conducted me to a dry lodge, where I remained until another one was erected over the old poles, when they returned for me again.

As the storm continued all day, accompanied by

snow and sleet, I remained inside talking with the people and taking notes. Crowds of Indians, of all ages, from the old, gray-headed warrior down to the little, tottering pappoose, gathered around me in amazement, wondering how the white man could put upon paper what he had seen and heard among their people.

One day I saw an Indian abuse his wife shamefully, striking her in the face and kicking her in the breast. The screams of the squaw soon brought a crowd around her, but no one offered to interfere, for a Sioux husband's power is absolute.

They parted with me reluctantly, still thinking that they could induce me to remain and live with them. Upon leaving, I was obliged to shake hands with every member of the different families with whom I had become intimately acquainted. I was expected to eat and smoke in every lodge. When about to leave a lodge, thinking that now I could slip away, some one from another tent, would come and say:

"The white man must come and have meat and coffee with us before he goes."

While among the Sioux, I was obliged to smoke their pipes with them, in order to gain their esteem and goodwill, though I never indulge in the habit outside of an Indian camp.

Leaving the village at last, I shaped my course eastward, and reached Niobrara in due time.

CHAPTER XV.

In the bosom of the valley,
Distant from the white man's home,
There in childish glee and freedom
The Indian children roam.

A. H. G.

AROUND THE LODGE FIRE WITH MY SIOUX FRIENDS—A GOOD OLD CHIEF—I RETURN TO SPOTTED TAIL'S CAMP—HOW AN INDIAN TELLS WHERE HE WAS BORN—I AM GIVEN A NEW NAME—BELLOWING BUFFALO—A GRASS DANCE—FAST DOG'S ACCOUNT OF THE OVERLAND MAIL ROBBERY—SPOTTED TAIL DIVIDES THE MONEY—FAST DOG SHOOK HANDS WITH THE WHITES AS THE REST WERE SHOOTING INTO THEM—BLACK CROW—IN A SNOW STORM—A RIDE BEHIND HIGH SHIELD— AN INDIAN FAMILY MOVING—FOUR-LEGGED BED-FELLOWS— HOW I REFUSED A MARRIAGE WITH A DUSKY MAID WHOSE MOTHER WANTED A WHITE SON—A PET DOG—BIG TURKEY— SCENES ON PONCA PRAIRIE—REFLECTIONS.

IN a few weeks after reaching the settlement, I again journeyed to the Sioux country, going in the interest of Professor Haldeman, who engaged me to obtain from the Sioux, certain stone implements of war and domestic use, for his donation to the Academy of Natural Sciences, at Philadelphia.

I stopped one night in a lodge with a family that I had met a year before, while traveling among the same tribe. During the evening we spent several hours in conversation, before retiring, and as usual when seated around the evening fire with my dusky friends, I was happy and contented.

The chief of the Yankton Sioux is Strike-the-Ree. He is an old man, and for years has not been on the war-path against the whites, but on several occasions, within late years, some of his braves joined other bands in their raids upon the whites.

Leaving the Yanktons, I went to Spotted Tail's village again, and experienced a long and tiresome journey over prairies and bluffs, and across ravines and dry creek beds.

While looking for Brave Bull's tent, I was hailed by Bellowing Buffalo, who had seen me in the camp while on my previous visit. He invited me into his lodge, where his wife presented me a pair of handsomely beaded buckskin leggins.

In the evening, a very old squaw came in, and in a little while, several others entered who appeared to be much younger. They were all surprised to find a white man in the camp, and were somewhat alarmed, thinking that I was a spy from some fort. When I called the old woman "e-nah-tahn-kah," or grandmother, they became more friendly.

The old squaw informed me that she was born near the Falls of the Missouri, many years before, and that she was the grandmother of the squaws who were with her, they being married and having grown children.

About the first questions an Indian asks a friend, are, "Where are you from? Have you a wife and children? Are your parents living? When did you

leave home?" They answer all such questions as
freely as they ask them.

They generally designate the place of their birth
by the position of rivers and mountains, which they
draw very accurately.

Bellowing Buffalo, desiring to give me an Indian
name, declared that I should be known as, "Wee
Ton-kah," or High Sun. He was led to name me
thus from the fact that it was noon when I arrived
at his tent, or when the sun was on the meridian,
according to the Indian method of reckoning the
time of mid-day.

In the evening, I visited the lodge of Fast Dog,
and after disposing of a dishful of boiled corn, and
smoking the "peace-pipe" which he had carried to
Washington when on a trip to see the President, I
accompanied him to a neighboring dance-lodge, in
order to see the braves perform the grass-dance.

This dance resembled all the others that I had
seen, with this exception, however: Each warrior,
upon entering the lodge, placed a small bunch of
grass over the top of two forked sticks, which had
been previously driven into the ground.

When I became weary of hearing the whoops of
the dancers, I returned to the lodge of Bellowing
Buffalo to sleep, as I had promised to do before I
left. The family had already retired, but a bed of
robes had been prepared for me, and I lay down
to sleep without a thought of fear.

The next day I returned to Fast Dog's lodge, as he had expressed a desire to have a talk with me. He informed me that he had never killed a white man, or stolen a white man's horse. I did not dispute his assertion, but I had other opinions.

According to his account, when Spotted Tail and his followers were shooting into the whites of the Overland Mail Coach, on the Platte River, some years ago, he did all he could to prevent them, and when he found that Spotted Tail was determined to shoot as long as one white man remained alive, he went among the whites and shook hands with them, so as to convince them that if they all fell under the fire of his companions, he alone was a friend as far as it was possible for him to be one.

After all the white men were killed, Spotted Tail broke open the money-box, and retaining some of the coin for himself, shared the remainder among his braves. Fast Dog and his family watched me earnestly as I noted down what he told me, and as I finished writing, he said: "Make a paper out of that, and make every one who reads it give you a dollar, some sugar, coffee and tobacco."

In this lodge I met a young black man who had lived among the Sioux since childhood. He was dressed like the Indians, spoke their language and took part in their dances and ceremonies. He was a favorite among the Sioux, and was known by the name of Black Crow.

After leaving this camp, which consisted of the Wash-ah-zah band of the Sioux nation, I started for the main Brule village, situated about fifteen miles further up the Ponca, twenty miles from its confluence with the Missouri.

It was now the beginning of May, and the day previous was warm and pleasant, but during the night, as is often the case in Dakota and Nebraska, at this time of the year, the weather changed very suddenly, growing quite cold.

In the morning some sleet fell, and the sky was dark and threatening, but I concluded to pursue my journey, hoping that the storm would soon be over. A short time after leaving camp, snow fell in great, blinding flakes, and soon the grass and flowers were covered with a mantle of white.

After traveling a few miles up the valley, I saw an Indian riding toward me. When he came up, he informed me that his family was moving up to the camp, and having lost his ax, he had returned to hunt it. After some parleying, he allowed me to ride behind him on his pony, but he insisted upon carrying my revolver until the village was reached, for an Indian is not at ease while an armed white man is behind him.

We rode a nimble little pony, and as the Indian was eager to overtake his family, we went over the ground at a rapid rate. When obliged to cross the bluffs, or descend the steep declivities of the ever-

winding Ponca, it was astonishing to me how very
sure-footed and cautious the pony was.

Upon reaching the summit of a hill that lay in
our course, the loud neighing of the pony informed
us that we were near the moving party, and soon
we came in sight of the caravan.

A number of Indians on the move is a singular
sight. A conveyance for transporting household
goods, babies, old and infirm people, pet dogs, etc.,
is made by securing a lodge-pole to each side of a
pony, leaving one end of them trail on the ground.
Across these poles two pieces of wood are tied, in
order to keep them from spreading, and the space
between the poles is then covered with raw-hide,
thus forming a convenient receptacle.

The trails made by a large party traveling this
way, are frequently worn to a depth of ten or more
inches; as the ponies travel in single file, the poles
constantly drag in one furrow. These trails resemble those made by buffaloes when traveling toward
water courses.

By the time the village was reached, I was wet
to the skin from the snow and sleet that had melted
on my clothes. My companion, whose name was
High Shield, conducted me to the lodge of one of
his friends, where we dried our clothes and obtained
dinner, while his poor, patient wife and his mother
erected the lodge, exposed to the storm. Much as
I pitied them, I would hardly have been allowed

to render them the assistance they so much needed.

In the evening, after taking supper with High Shield, we visited his twin brother, Long Pumpkin. These two Indians, together with Medicine Lake, Brave Bull, Bellowing Buffalo, Spotted Eagle and Cherry Stone, were the best friends I had among the Sioux Indians. They became warmly attached to me, and were always ready to befriend me, and the shelter of their lodges, the use of their ponies and weapons, were ever at my disposal.

That night, while stopping in High Shield's tent, his wife put a raw-hide net at the head of my bed, in order to keep the dogs from entering at a rent in the lodge at that place. But they would not be kept in the cold, and found some other way to get into the lodge. Having been awakened from sleep by the movement of something on my bed, I found a huge dog lying by my side, while another one was trying to creep beneath the blankets. The night being too cold and stormy to compel even a dog to sleep out, I shared my couch with them.

One of Big Star's wives wanted to give me her sixteen-year-old daughter for a wife, but I declined to accept her kind offer, and informed her that the daughter was too young, that I was a sedate, old-fashioned young man, that I liked old women best and, moreover, I had no desire to taste the bliss of married life until I had seen more of the world, To this the mother said:

"She will get old soon enough, and you should see how she can work, and what nice leggins she can make."

In the estimation of the mother, this was a fair argument in the daughter's favor, but I evaded the contract the mother desired.

The next day I visited an eccentric old warrior named Two Elks. He had a little pet dog that seemed to understand every word he spoke to it. The dog had a buckskin robe, which was covered with bead-work. The old man was a much greater curiosity than either the dog or its blanket, and, in all probability, he was the only peculiarity of this kind in the world. The Indians declared that he became a raving maniac whenever a strange woman entered his lodge. There are, without a doubt, no small number of white married ladies who would be glad to see their truant husbands become insane at the sight of a strange woman.

While seated in a wigwam one day, Big Turkey, the Indian who killed Sergeant Dougherty on the Loup Fork of the Platte River, a few years ago, came in and greeted me warmly. I did not like his countenance, and was cautious in my conversation with him.

One day I walked out to the bluffs overlooking the valley and surrounding country. The storm had passed over a week before, and all Nature now seemed to rejoice at the change. The valley, plains and bluffs, were covered with a carpet of green, and the prairie violet and honey-suckle were just beginning to bud.

As far as the eye could see, up or down the river, were the tall, white wigwams, forming a striking contrast to the deep green of the valley and hills around them, while in the east and west were vast chains of bluffs, between whose ridges were little valleys, or meadows, opening into the greater one of Ponca River.

The Indian village was romantically situated in the bosom of the valley, the sparkling little Ponca continually winding through it. As I stood upon the topmost bluff and gazed around me, a mighty expanse of waving grass, resembling the ocean, met my view.

I could see the surrounding country for miles in extent. What a glorious sight lay before me! A view to make the soul expand with lofty thoughts and sentiments, and to cause the frail tenement to sink into insignificance before its splendor.

On all sides were the lovely prairies, bluffs and valleys, covered with beautiful grass and budding flowers in all the glory of enchanting spring-time.

Far away toward the eastern horizon, was the swift-flowing Niobrara, whose course was marked out by the belt of timber that lined its banks, and in the north were to be seen the high chalk-stone bluffs, between whose rugged sides was confined the muddy, turbulent Missouri. I stood and noted all with the poetical emotions of pleasant melancholy, which the majestic scenery of the West ever awakens in the breast of the lover of Nature.

As I looked over the Indian village in the valley below, these thoughts came to my mind: "Soon all will be changed! The pioneer's plow will overturn the prairie sod, and his drill will deposit the grains of wheat and corn soon to spring up instead of the prairie grass and flowers. The white man's substantial house will take the place of the Indian wigwam, and the puffing iron-horse, bringing with it the commerce and luxuries of civilization, will thunder through the valley now occupied by the Indian village."

Many times I have thus stood on the grand hills and plains of the West, far from the contentions and vanities of civilization, with heart and mind enchanted by the marvelous beauty of this strange, bewildering country.

CHAPTER XVI.

. las. for them! their day is nearly o'er
.ar fires recede toward the Western shore;
ir children look, by power oppressed,
. eyond the mountains of the West.

AXON

PETRIFIED WOOD ON THE PRAIRIES—SORREL HORSE—A WILD
SQUAW—SITTING BULL—I VISIT TWO STRIKE AND SPOTTED
TAIL—HOW THE GREAT CHIEFS LOOK AND LIVE AT THEIR
HOMES—I AT LAST BECOME WEARY OF THE INDIAN LIFE—
SIOUX MOURNING FOR THEIR DEAD—KINDNESS OF CHERRY
STONE—BEAR-THAT-LOOKS-BEHIND—A SQUAW ONE HUNDRED
AND THIRTY YEARS OLD—A SINGULAR SIGHT—FRIENDS IN
TIME OF NEED—'IONORED WITH A FEAST OF DOG'S MEAT—
A PONCA INDIAN GRAVE YARD—ALONE WITH THE DEAD—
MY ADVENTURE WITH A SKELETON—A SOLEMN THOUGHT—
A HOME ON THE WESTERN PRAIRIES—HOW TO OBTAIN AN
EXCELLENT FARM IN THE WEST FOR FOURTEEN DOLLARS.

IN many places on the prairies, far from timber
of any kind, are found petrified wood and bones
in great quantities.   These singular remains of bygone centuries, seem to substantiate the theory of
scientific men who say that the plains of the West
were once the bottom of a vast inland sea.   There
is also an Indian tradition to the effect that a great
body of water once rolled over the country.

Sorrel Horse, a son-in-law of Two Strike, came
into a lodge where I was one night, but the family
did not seem to like him, and although we were

taking supper at the time, the people of the lodge did not invite him to join us. As all the rest thus slighted him, I gave him half the contents of my plate, and began a conversation with him.

My attention appeared to make him thoughtful, but he said nothing about it at the time. It was easy to see that he was pleased, as well as affected. About an hour later, after having left the lodge, he came in and handed me a choice piece of meat.

He had promised to see me safe to Two Strike's camp, the next morning, so when I was ready to go I went in search of him, and found him engaged in a dance, but he left the group of warriors and accompanied me to the camp, about three or four miles further up the river.

We were frequently obliged to cross the stream over huge trees that had been cut down in such a manner, that they fell lengthwise across the narrow river, and formed good foot-bridges.

The wife of Sorrel Horse saw us coming, and at once began to prepare food for us. Entering the lodge, he spread a buffalo-robe for me to sit upon. I gave him a few blank pages from my diary to draw some pictures upon, and when he had completed them, he presented them to me, saying that I should take them home with me.

One of these drawings represent Sorrel Horse hunting buffaloes, surprising his enemies and stampeding their ponies. Another shows the interior of his tent, his wife making moccasins, and myself watching the process.

While seated in the lodge, an old squaw entered with an ax in hand, and seeing me, rushed toward me instantly with the ax raised above her head, as though she intended to strike me. Grasping a gun that lay at my side, I presented it toward her, and was compelled to strike her in the breast with the muzzle of it before she desisted. She then went out of the lodge immediately.

I had never seen the squaw before, and what her intention was, I could not learn, for Sorrel Horse was silent, and would give me no explanation. I supposed that she belonged to either the party of Crazy Horse or Roman Nose, many of whom had joined the Brules shortly after the Custer battle, and that having lost some friends in the fight, she had concluded to find revenge by killing me.

Sitting Bull, chief of the Unkpapa Sioux, is described as being of medium height and well built, though slightly bow-legged. The expression of his countenance is fierce and cruel. He has a full face, prominent nose, massive jaw-bones, piercing, blood-shot black eyes and large perceptive organs. He is said to have been born near Spirit Lake, Iowa, about the year 1835.

Approaching the lodge of Two Strike, I found the chief seated on the ground in front of it, with a little group of his warriors. After smoking for a

few minutes with the party, he conducted me into
his tent, where he showed me some photographs
of himself that had been taken in Washington, by
Alexandria Gardener, of 921 Pennsylvania Avenue.
He also had a card of Cornell & Amerman, dry-
good merchants at 79 Leonard Street, New York,
and a report of the council held by the President
and the visiting Indian chiefs of the Sioux nation,
at Washington, in September, 1877.

These things, which had been given to him while
he was in the East, he had carefully tied up in an
old calico rag, and seemed to prize them highly.

Two Strike went with me to the tent of Spotted
Tail, about three miles distant. Nearing the lodge,
we found the great chief at the door watching the
young men engaged in horse-racing. He grasped
my hand warmly, and after a few passing remarks,
we entered his lodge, where we had some meat and
a smoke.

According to Spotted Tail's account, and the cal-
culations I made from it, he was born about 1823,
near the source of the Niobrara River, and became
a chief when in his twenty-eighth year. He is tall
and straight, but rather slender, and finer featured
than the Indians generally are. He is quiet and
reserved, and the general expression of his face is
mild and genial, but his closed lips indicate great
decision, while his deep, thoughtful eyes betoken a
reserve will-power.

At the time of my visit, he had four wives and twelve children. His main tent was an extra large one, and was better furnished, in the way of robes, cooking utensils, etc., than the lodges of the other Indians. The chief was about the most neglected-looking object about the place, his dress consisting of the indispensable breech-cloth, an old shirt, and coarse moccasins that no longer completely covered his feet.

In answer to my inquiry as to how he obtained his name, he said:

"My father's name was 'Wild Cat,' and when I was a little boy, an old white trapper, who used to visit our village, said that because I was a young 'Wild Cat,' he would name me after a small part of a wild-cat. So, as the tail, which is spotted, is a small part of the animal, he said that I should be known as 'Spotted Tail.'"

He informed me that he had been at war with all of his enemies, and when I asked him whether he had killed many of his foes, he said: "Yes, or I could not have become a chief and remained one." Both Two Strike and Spotted Tail, gave me one of their photographs which had been taken while the chiefs were in Washington.

Every day there were ball games, foot races, bow and arrow trials and feasts, and half the hours of night were occupied by wild dances and the howls and groans of the "medicine men," so that I at last became weary of Indian life, and wished myself in civilization again.

A number of deaths occurred while I was among these Indians, and the lamentations of the friends of the deceased were both horrid and affecting. A child died one day in a lodge near the one in which I was stopping, and I was made aware of the fact as I entered the village, by seeing the body lying outside of the lodge, wrapped in a blanket. The friends of the child passed the night on the bluffs, near by, weeping in the most heart-rending manner.

On my way back to the Missouri I was overtaken by a rain storm, while near one of the Brule camps. I was quite wet by the time I reached the village, and upon entering a lodge, I informed the Indians that I desired the shelter of their tent. The owner, who proved to be Cherry Stone, at once welcomed me to a seat on a blanket, near the fire.

In the evening I passed a pleasant time with the family and the other Indians who came to see me. Cherry Stone and his wife gave me several Indian relics to take east with me.

The next morning, after passing the night with Cherry Stone, I rode with him to White Thunder's village, where I visited an old warrior named Bear-that-Looks-Behind. As he was an old gray-headed man, I asked him how old he was, and he said that he had seen eighty-five snows.

He then conducted me to a little, old, weather-

beaten lodge, which was no more than five feet in
diameter. It was so low that I could look in at the
top where the poles met, and such a sight as met
my view, I never saw before, and in all probability,
I will never see the like again. Seated on a buffalo
robe, was the bony figure of a woman, bent almost
double, and having just enough flesh on the frame
to convince me that the object was not a skeleton
over which a parchment sack had been drawn.

This was the old man's mother, and when he informed her that the white man was there, she put
her skeleton-like hand through a rent in the lodge,
and greeted me in a voice scarcely audible. Then
her eighty-five-year-old son crawled into the lodge,
and bade me follow him, for the rain was falling in
torrents at the time.

The lodge was just large enough to hold us in a
stooping posture, and, upon leaving, we were compelled to back out on our hands and knees. The
old squaw and her pet dog were both sitting upon
the same fur-bed, and a dishful of meat and some
water had been placed within her reach. Some fire
was smouldering in the center of the lodge when
we entered, but as the smoke pained my eyes, the
old man extinguished it.

The little patch of hair on her head was entirely
white, while her face and limbs appeared to be but
skin and bone. As I looked upon her shrunken
frame, in which it seemed almost impossible for life

to exist, the thought occurred to me that she had lived to see generation after generation come and go, while she still remained, pent up in a little coop because her days of usefulness were over.

I had deemed her son to be venerable, but when I saw the mother and her son together, the wide contrast in their appearance was truly amazing, and I fancied the old gray-headed man looked boyish. The squaw informed me that she was born near a stream that rises in the Black Hills, and that her name was Wah-ol-lie.

According to her own account, as well as that of her son and all the other old Indians I questioned concerning her, she had reached the almost unparalleled age of one hundred and thirty years. If this statement is true, she must have been born in 1748, before the Revolutionary War, and when the Atlantic States were yet inhabited by Indians.

Incredible as this may appear, I believe it to be correct, and could the reader have seen that emaciated, mummy-like, unearthly looking figure, he also would agree with me.

Before leaving, she informed me that a donation toward buying some goods for a new dress, when some of her people could visit the traders, would be acceptable. So I gave her money to purchase the first female garment of which I ever had the honor of being the author.

One bright, sunny morning, after a farewell visit

to Good Wash, Bellowing Buffalo and Fast Dog, I started for the Niobrara Settlement. As I stood upon the bluffs overlooking the vast Indian camps, on my departure, and looked for the last time upon these strange, interesting people to whom I had become so singularly attached, and among whom I had ever found hospitality and protection, feelings akin to sorrow and regret came over me.

My route, between the Ponca and Niobrara, lay over a succession of high bluffs, dry creek beds and rugged ravines. As I had a heavy load of Indian relics to carry upon my back, the journey was very fatiguing. Between some of the hills were delightful little valleys, through which flowed tiny streams of pure, delicious water, that gave life and vigor to the vegetation around, and formed a pleasant relief for the eyes weary of looking upon sand hills and sage-brush.

During the journey a rain storm arose, and for several hours, I was obliged to face it. As I came to a creek, near its confluence with the Missouri, I was greeted by the welcome sight of several Sioux lodges, on a little plat of ground near the creek.

Foot-sore, weary, hungry and wet to the skin, I quickened my pace, urged onward by the prospect of shelter. Upon entering one of the tents, I was invited to a seat near the fire. I noticed that the squaws were boiling meat, and soon I, with all the other inmates of the lodge, was given some of it.

Seeing that the flesh was that of some small animal. I asked them what it was, and they smilingly
replied that it was a young antelope which one of
the warriors had shot. But after I had eaten some
of it, the Indians began to laugh, and then asked
me how I liked dog's meat.

I now comprehended the joke they had played
upon me. but as I was very hungry, and the meat
being savory, I proceeded with the repast.

When the rain ceased, I continued on my route,
and during the afternoon I reached a Ponca Indian
grave-yard, where I examined a number of graves.
This place of burial was situated on a high bluff,
within a stone's cast of the Missouri and overlooking the surrounding country for miles.

I found the bodies in a sitting posture, with the
face toward the East. No earth had been placed
upon them, the covering being robes and blankets.
A small roof of limbs and bark had been erected
over the graves, and by removing these, or looking
through the crevices, the bodies could be seen.

Although the Indians embalm the bodies of the
dead, the flesh finally wastes away. In one grave I
found a huge, grinning skeleton, sitting upright as
it had been placed. The covering of blankets had
decayed and crumbled to dust, and nothing but a
naked skeleton remained. The limbs were almost
covered with cups and dishes that had contained
food and water, which the Poncas had placed there

for the accommodation of the spirit, on its visit to the body. These Indians believe that the spirits of the deceased return to view the body, and partake of the food which is prepared for them.

The upper part of the skull was covered with a turban, which did not have the decayed appearance of the other contents of the grave. My curiosity being aroused at this, I touched the skull with my walking-stick, when lo! it fell from the bony frame with a dull, heavy sound and rolled among the old cups and dishes.

Becoming alarmed at my movements, and fearing that they would lead me into trouble, I started to leave, when to my surprise, I saw a Ponca boy, who had dismounted from his pony, examining my bundle of Sioux relics, which I had left a few hundred yards from the grave-yard.

As he was interested in the relics, he did not see me, and I instantly took advantage of this to leave the graves. He soon mounted his horse and took my bundle along with him, but I hailed him, when he stopped and waited until I got up to him.

He was somewhat surprised to find a white man there alone, but I told him that I was no stranger to his people, that I had been to Spotted Tail's village and was now on my way to the settlement.

So we parted friendly, he promising to carry my package on to the Niobrara River, where he lived. Upon reaching the river, about an hour afterward, I found a number of Poncas encamped on its bank, and my relics were handed to me by one of them.

While there alone with the dead, and seeing what we must all come to—a mere handful of repulsive clay and ashes—the utter hollowness and delusion of this world, with its riches, honors and pride, was most vividly presented to my mind. A very forcible truth was shown me by the grinning skeletons and mouldering bodies, which, a short time before, had been full of life and activity.

I found the river so high and turbulent that I could not cross it in a canoe, so I was compelled to return to the mouth of the Ponca, where I crossed the Missouri, and then journeyed to the settlement by another route. After a short stay in Niobrara, I went down to Yankton, and then proceeded on to my home in Pennsylvania.

A few years ago, the country between Yankton and Niobrara was but a tract of wild prairie, but marvelous changes have since taken place. Good farms and buildings have appeared with a rapidity that is wonderful.

A few miles back from the river, there is plenty of Government land to be obtained. All that is required in order to get a farm in the West for the sum of fourteen dollars, is to have the chosen tract surveyed, and then entered at the land-office of the district in which the land lies, pay the fees, which are the fourteen dollars, and then improve the land.

CHAPTER XVII.

In Dixie Land I take my stand,
To live and die in Dixie Land.

Away down South in the fields of cotton,
Persimmon seeds and a sandy bottom.

            •   ANON.

BOUND FOR FLORIDA—PETERSBURG—SOUTHERN WAR RELICS—
WELDON—PICKING THE COTTON—THE SOUTHERN PEOPLE—
HOW PEA-NUTS GROW—A RABBIT TRAP—A HERO OF THE
CONFEDERACY—PINE FORESTS OF THE SOUTH—MY CAMP
FIRE AMONG THE PINES—A THOUGHT FOR THE FUTURE—
WILMINGTON—AN OLD PLANTATION SCENE—THE FLORENCE
WAR-PRISON—A LADY, DISGUISED AS A MAN, GOES TO WAR
WITH HER HUSBAND AND DIES IN PRISON—THE NATIONAL
CEMETERY—CHARLESTON—BEAUTY OF SOUTHERN LADIES—
SAVANNAH—A SOUTHERN POOR MAN'S HOME—THE STATION
IN LIFE WHICH AFFORDS THE MOST HAPPINESS—A CURIOUS
PRINTING-PRESS—A LADY WHOSE KNOWLEDGE OF MEN AND
THE WORLD WAS LIMITED—A PRETTY, BUT STERN, WIDOW
WHO DID NOT LIKE "YANKEES"—TIME HEALS ALL SORROW.

AFTER staying at home a few months, I started
for Florida in the interest of Professor Haldeman,
who employed me to explore some of the ancient
Indian mounds, in order to obtain antiquities for
his collection.

Going by way of York, Baltimore, Washington
and Richmond, I, in due time, reached Petersburg,
Virginia. This city is located on the Appomattox
River, and is a harbor for light-draught ships. The

place figured prominently during the war, as the remaining breast-works near the city indicate.

Weldon, on the Roanoke River, is a small town surrounded by vast pine forests. Like Petersburg, it had a fair share of soldiers and skirmishes to endure at the time of the Rebellion.

Between Petersburg and Weldon the cotton-belt begins, and groups of merry, colored folks, of both sexes, old and young, are to be seen gliding along between the rows of cotton, picking the spotless product into baskets, while they sing their home-made songs, and jest with all the vigor, and in the idioms peculiar to the race.

Persimmons abound throughout the South, but very little use is made of them by the people, still, when properly dried, they are not inferior to dates.

Pea-nuts are very productive in the Carolinas, and form a profitable crop. They are planted and cultivated similar to the string-bean. The stalks also resemble those of the string-bean. When ripe, the stalks are pulled up and stacked like hay. After the roots, to which the nuts adhere, are dry, the process of picking commences.

A favorite sport of the colored people is catching rabbits and opossums by means of a trap called a gum. This trap generally consists of a piece of a hollow log, about two feet in length, and closed at one end, while at the other is the trap-door.

At Warsaw, North Carolina, I stopped one night

with a gentleman who had taken part in the Battle of Gettysburg, on the Confederate side, and though he had lost an arm there, he had a good opinion of the Northern people.

In the evening, as we sat before the blazing fire of resinous pine, joined by his accomplished lady and interesting children, many old and interesting reminiscences of the war were related by my host, and the doings of both "Yankees" and "Rebels," were good-naturedly related.

An important industry of North Carolina is the manufacture of rosin, turpentine, tar and pitch, the product of the pine tree. The shipment of these articles from Wilmington to Northern and foreign ports is very large.

Some of the pine forests of the South are very beautiful. The trees are lofty and straight, many of them not having a single crook for a distance of fifty feet from the ground. Some places the surface is quite level, and covered with a fine growth of wire-grass, giving the forest the appearance of a well-regulated park.

While hunting Indian mounds, I often camped in these pineries at night, and slept on a bed made of wire-grass and branches of young trees, beside a blazing fire of pine faggots.

Often, as I sat alone by my camp-fire, preparing my frugal meal of roasted sweet-potatoes, packing Indian relics, or taking notes, my thoughts would dwell upon the singular inclinations that prompted me to lead such a roving life.

As the hooting of the lonely night-owl sounded through the woods, and the wind sighed dreamily through the pines, causing a singular melancholy feeling to steal over me, I would mentally ask myself this question: "Will I, when all my traveling and hardships are over, be so fortunate as to settle down successfully, and have a happy, comfortable home of my own—a haven of peace and contentment. in this struggling, tumultuous world?"

Wilmington, North Carolina, is a seaport town, and, like Charleston and Savannah, it does a large shipping trade with American and European ports. The city contains many handsome residences, which are surrounded by grounds tastefully arranged and cultivated. The people are very sociable, kind and frank, and the traveler leaves them with regret.

One night, while at Flemington, North Carolina, my attention was attracted by the sound of a banjo and the shuffling of feet, in a cabin near by. Upon entering the place, I found a colored man playing a banjo and singing an old plantation song, while another was dancing to the time of the music, surrounded by twenty or thirty other black men and boys, all in a high state of excitement.

They made room for me by the fire as I entered, and when I asked them to present one of the most popular scenes on "de old plantation," during the days of slavery, they cleared a wider space, and for the next hour, they danced and sang as these black folks only can.

There was a singular and ludicrous mingling of half-naked legs, woolly heads, rolling eye-balls and glittering teeth, that I never saw before. The glare of the fire, and the waving pine torches that were held by some of the dancers, added a grotesque, weird appearance to the whole scene.

On leaving the place, I promised to mention the affair in print. This pleased them very much, and one of them exclaimed: "Dat's right sah! I am York Williams!"

Near Florence, South Carolina, is the noted war prison where so many Northern prisoners of war were confined during the Rebellion. The prison, which at the time of my visit remained about as it had been when containing the prisoners, was but a large tract of sandy low-land, encircled by a stockade, on the outside of which was a deep trench.

Mrs. Florena Budwin, a Northern lady, who was unwilling to have her husband enter the army and leave her at home, accompanied him, disguised as a man. In course of time, they, with other Union soldiers, were captured by the Confederates, and confined at Andersonville, Georgia.

When a number of the Andersonville prisoners were transferred to Florence, Mrs. Budwin was one of the number, but her husband was not. Being loath to make known their relation, Mrs. Budwin left, and her husband remained. They never met again, for Mr. Budwin died soon after they parted.

The lady's disguise was so. perfect, that her sex was not known until sometime after she had been at Florence, when she died in confinement.

Half a mile from the stockade is the grave-yard, where the bodies of three thousand Northern men were buried. The Government has since built a fine brick wall around the cemetery, and erected a white marble tomb-stone to the memory of each of the men, as well as otherwise beautified the place.

A large flag waves from a staff, near the foot of which is a conical-shaped heap of cannon balls, and a little further on, like grim sentinels, stand two huge cannons, in an upright position. The whole aspect of the place tends to fill the visitor with a feeling of awe and solemnity.

A rose-bush, larger and finer than any other in the cemetery, blossoms and blooms over the grave that contains the remains of Florena Budwin and her babe. Died in a distand land, far from home and friends; how sad to contemplate!

A gentleman from Philadelphia was appointed by the Government to take care of the cemetery. He has a comfortable brick house in the enclosure, and receives a salary of a thousand dollars a year.

Approaching the city of Charleston, a very fine section of bottom land is reached, which produces

strawberries, peas, beans, etc., in March and April.
There are also many enchanting groves of grand
old live-oak trees, enveloped in fanciful wreaths,
fringes and veils, of the beautiful Spanish, or gray,
hanging-moss.

Charleston is a city of which the Southerners are
proud, but the people, more than any other feature
of the city, call forth the praise and admiration of
the traveler. Some of the most thoroughly kind,
hospitable, unselfish people I ever met, were these
Charlestonians.

The dwellings have a luxurious, home-like aspect
about them, and are most delightfully embowered
in groves and clusters of orange, lemon, magnolia
and other tropical trees. The inhabitants are very
refined, well educated and courteous.

The South has always been noted for the beauty
of its ladies, and while I do not admire beauty of
face or form, near so much as I do female cheerfulness of disposition, kindness of heart and plain,
unassuming manner of dress, speech and general
deportment, I heartily admire the charming ladies
of Charleston for the fulness in which they possess
all these features of loveliness.

In addition to beautiful parks which adorn the
city, the Battery forms a grand promenade, from
which the docks and shipping present an interesting sight. The population is fifty-four thousand.

The Southern pine is much stronger impregnated

with rosin than that found in California, or in the pine sections of Minnesota, Wisconsin, Michigan and Pennsylvania, and it makes a hotter and more lasting fire, and is more easily ignited. Wood that contains a fair portion of rosin, is said to be "fat."

As a consequence of the universal use of pine as fuel in the South, the old-fashioned fire-place, fire-dogs and tongs, still remain household necessities. In the country, the rooms of the poor people are often illuminiated by a pine torch, placed in some convenient nook or corner.

Between Charleston and Savannah are immense deposits of petrified bones, of both land and sea monsters. Within late years these deposits have been utilized. Many mills are engaged in grinding the substance, after which it is mixed with certain chemicals, and sold for fertilizing purposes.

I was shown over the Wando Phosphate Works, about ten miles from Charleston, by the foreman of the place. Here I found bones of animals of mammoth size, also tusks, sharks' teeth, etc.

At Jacksonborough, South Carolina, I passed a day very pleasantly with a late Charleston newspaper man. He was a representative type of the generous-hearted, sociable Southern gentleman, and were he not as modest of himself and works as the retired journalist is, I would take the liberty to say more about him and his estimable family.

For twenty years he had been a hard-working

newspaper man, and at the age of fifty he retired
from the field, longing to leave the din and bustle
of the city, as well as the manifold cares incident
to a journalistic life.

In the afternoon, we drove into the country, and
passed through a fine forest of pine and live-oak,
through which wound a grand, avenue-like road, on
each side of which were tall trees, covered with a
mantle of gray moss, hanging in graceful, waving
clusters and ringlets.

Continuing southward, I reached Savannah, one
of the most beautiful cities in the South. Nearly
all of the squares contain a delightful little park,
and fine shade trees grow along both sides of the
streets, giving the city a very pleasing appearance.
Here, as in all the other Southern cities, much care
and attention is given to the cultivation of yards,
lawns, gardens and flower beds, which speaks well
for the taste of the people. While the exterior of
their homes are thus adorned with things pleasing
to the eye, the interior is embellished with the good
and pure in art and literature.

Those refined, poetic souls who find in the field,
sky and sea, or in art and literature, beauties that
call forth their love and devotion, have a heart and
mind elevated far above the pride, selfishness and
avarice, of the small-souled, narrow-minded beings
of earth, and live in a sphere of inward peace and
happiness unknown to the giddy and thoughtless.

Savannah lies on the Savannah River, eighteen miles from the ocean. It is a large cotton market, and it also does an extensive trade in lumber and ship-supplies. Like other coast cities of the South, it is connected with Baltimore, Philadelphia, New York and Boston, by regular lines of steamships. The population is about twenty-nine thousand.

While on my travels among strangers, and when dejected and weary of sight-seeing, a letter from home, or some distant friend, was an oasis to the mind. A kind missive, like a kind word, is, indeed, a soothing balm to the troubled and discouraged soul. It is prized as a precious emblem of friendship and affection, and tends to raise us above the petty cares and contentions of life.

Few pumps are seen in the country, and water is drawn by means of a very primitive apparatus. A post is driven into the ground, and upon the top of it is fastened a long, swinging shaft, much heavier at one end than at the other. To the light end, a bucket is tied, and the shaft is so balanced on the post, that the bucket can be let down into the well and drawn up full of water by a small child.

The home of the poor man, in the country, is not inferior to that of the Western pioneer, and it has some advantages over the latter. Wood for fuel, and timber for building, can, in many places, be had for the labor of cutting it. This, in addition to a mild climate and an abundance of water, are great advantages that many Western people do not have.

The houses of the poor people are usually built of logs. These dwellings generally have no more than one or two rooms, and no upper apartments. Each room is about fifteen feet long and twenty feet wide. In some parts of the South, the cost of building a house of this kind is but a few dollars.

All the cooking is done in a huge fire-place, the utensils being an iron pot, a frying-pan, coffee pot and Dutch oven. The winters are so mild that the doors are left open half the time. Southerners in the country, seldom lock their doors upon retiring to bed, and many of their doors are without lock and key. This is not occasioned by extreme carelessness or poverty, but simply because they have more faith and confidence in humanity than many other people have.

There was always something cheerful and fascinating to me in the bright, generous glow of a fire of pine wood in a Southern home, and some of the most pleasant acquaintances I formed while on my travels, were around the evening fire, in the South.

My rambles have brought me into the mansions of the wealthy and honored, and into the hovels of the poor and lowly, as well as into the abodes of the middle class, and I firmly believe that the last named class are by far the happiest. They are not annoyed by the many cares and temptations of the rich, nor the trials and poverty of the extremely poor, but having a fair portion of the necessaries of life, they dwell in a sphere of contentment and happiness, and seem to glide smoothly through life.

Between the Okefenoke Swamp, in Georgia, and the Florida line, is Du Pont, a small station on the Atlantic & Gulf Railroad. At the time of my visit to the place in December, 1878, it contained about thirty houses, and a printing-office, from which was issued the *Okefenokean*.

The press upon which the paper was printed was a curiosity. The form of type was placed on a flat stone, which rested on a pine table. The form was inked with a hand roller, and after the blank sheet was placed upon the type, a round pine log, with the bark off, and covered with a bed-blanket, was rolled over the form, and produced the impression.

Upon the press was printed various kinds of job-work, and, according to the brazen announcement of the editor, it was done "in the highest style of the art, and with neatness and despatch!" If this press had appeared in the fifteenth century, Laurentius, Gutenberg, Faust and Schœffer, inventors of "the art preservative," would, in all probability, have concluded that they were not the pioneers of the printing business.

Near Jasper, Florida, a lady whose knowledge of men and the world was limited, learning that I was a Pennsylvanian, eyed me sharply, and at the same time said that she had always deemed "Yankees" to be very large men, with red hair and blue eyes.

Some of the Southern folks, who lost slaves and other property during the war, have not a friendly feeling toward the Northerners, though, to a great extent, the old war-feeling of hatred and bitterness has died out.   ·

A very handsome little black-eyed widow, living in Suwanee, Florida, who, during the Rebellion had resided in great splendor in Savannah, said to me:

"Since the 'Yankees' robbed me of my home and slaves, I have been obliged to do all my own work, besides following the occupation of dress-maker as a means of supporting my little family. Had one of you 'Yankees' entered my house soon after the war, I would have broom-sticked you out, for then I hated the sight of a 'Yankee'. Time, however, which is the greatest healer of all our sorrows, has made me more lenient toward your people."

Some of the grand old pine forests of the South are natural parks of rare beauty, and many of them are still the home of bears, deer and other game.

Along the shores of the widely-sung "Suwanee River," in Florida, are to be found the petrified remains of mammoth land and water animals.

CHAPTER XVIII.

Florida, the beautiful " Land of Flowers,"
Of sunshine bright and blooming bowers;
Within whose pale of perpetual summer,
Is a home and a welcome for every comer.

We glance far down through the piney vales,
Where Spanish moss hangs in clusters and trails,
And magnolias bend in the cool sea breeze
That ever rustles among the palmetto-trees.

A. H G.

CHRISTMAS DAY IN FLORIDA—SUNSHINE AND FLOWERS—THE
FLORIDA CLIMATE—SWEET POTATOES—JACKSONVILLE—RIPE
STRAWBERRIES ON NEW YEAR'S DAY UNDER THE SHADE OF
ORANGE-TREES—ASPECT OF THE SOUTHERN GENTLEMAN'S
HOME—THE BANANA TREES—SPANISH, OR HANGING-MOSS—
AN ANCIENT INDIAN MOUND—FERNANDINA—THE BEACH—
THE PALM, OR PALMETTO-TREE AND PLANT—A PALMETTO
HOUSE—A CURIOUS PLACE FOR A HEN'S NEST—FORESTS OF
FLORIDA—HOME OF THE CACTUS AND CENTURY PLANTS—
AN ORANGE-GROVE—MY FRIENDS—THE OYSTER AT HOME—
A CANDY PULLING—INDIAN RELICS—THE COLORED FOLKS—
THE RACE CONSIDERED—WHY WON'T THE GOOD ONES GET
TO HEAVEN?—ORANGE BLOSSOMS—PARTING OF FRIENDS—
THE BOON OF TRUE FRIENDSHIP.

I REACHED Live Oak, Florida, on Christmas Eve,
and the following day I went over to Lake City, a
handsome place which received its name from the
beautiful little lakes in the vicinity. On each side
of the streets are rows of fine live-oak shade trees,
and in almost every yard and garden are clusters of
orange and banana trees, many of them towering

above the house-tops, and all bearing fruit in great abundance, and of fine quality.

It was both wonderful and enchanting to walk along the streets on Christmas and see the orange-trees bending under their weight of ripe, golden fruit, the roses in bloom, and the people sitting in the open air.

While Christmas Day in Florida was as pleasant and warm as a June day is in the Northern States, there were three feet of snow at Buffalo, and four inches at St. Louis and Cincinnati, while the great Mississippi River was ice-bound from St. Paul to the Kentucky line.

The winter weather of Florida resembles the delightful, balmy Indian Summer of the North. In Southern Florida, frost is a curiosity, and even as far north as the Georgia line, ice as thick as glass, seldom forms, and then only upon standing water in troughs, etc. Running water never freezes, and there are old men and women in Florida who never saw snow or ice.

Sweet potatoes are one of the principal crops of the soil, and form an important article of food for both rich and poor. They grow much larger and more abundantly here than they do in the North, and are of a much finer flavor.

From Lake City I went to Jacksonville. This is the largest city in Florida, and a favorite resort for Northern people who desire to escape the rigor of the Northern winter. It is a seaport town situated on the St. Johns River, about eighteen miles from the Atlantic. The population is twelve thousand.

The first day of January was warm and delightful, and under the shade of the orange-trees were ripe strawberries and vegetables. In the yards and gardens, in almost every part of the city, are to be seen the orange trees bending under their weight of yellow fruit. Unless plucked, some oranges always remain upon the trees until they blossom again for another crop.

Ice of an excellent quality is manufactured here by a chemical process, and large quantities are also shipped from the North.

Since the war, the Southern gentleman does not live in the state of ease and luxury which he once enjoyed. The groups of house and field negroes, formerly held as slaves, are no longer found in the capacity of such, though they still linger about the old home that sheltered them long before the days of freedom, the stately abode of the once princely planter has a dilapidated aspect, and the dazzling splendor, wealth and gaiety, that reigned supreme within the palatial mansion, are, to a great extent, things of the past.

Notwithstanding all this reverse of fortune, the Southern lady and gentleman are, in general, kind, genial and hospitable to all, and the Northern man who travels among them must be small-souled and narrow-minded, if he fails to realize that a sad and unnecessary desolation was brought upon an excellent and generous people by his own countrymen.

Bananas are grown in all parts of Florida. The tree upon which they grow is from eight to twenty feet high, and is of but one year's growth, as the tree, or rather its branches, die soon after the crop has been gathered, but the roots retain life, and the following season, give birth to another tree.

In Florida, as well as in other Southern States, is found the pretty Spanish, or hanging-moss. It is of a grayish color, and is from four to eighteen inches in length. It sometimes covers the trees like a mantle, hanging in graceful, waving clusters from the branches. The forests are often thus adorned for miles in extent, the trees, at a distance, resembling those of a Northern forest when coated with snow or ice.

This moss is extensively used in the manufacture of mattresses, sofas, etc., and it is almost equal to hair for the purpose. It grows suspended in the air from the branches of trees, receiving no nutriment from the earth, and being destitute of roots. The Southern ladies decorate their parlors with it, and it seems to thrive there as well as it does upon the trees, presenting a beautiful and rustic effect.

In a large pine forest, owned by Mr. M. Burney, living near Callahan, Florida, I opened an ancient Indian mound. It was about four feet above the level of the ground, and over a hundred feet in circumference. On the top of the mound was a pine tree about two feet thick at the trunk, the roots of which were a great annoyance to me while opening the sepulchre, and I found a small root growing in the hollow of a man's leg-bone.

Several feet from the top of the mound, I found a number of human bones in an advanced state of decay, also some red clay pottery. At one place I dug up a skull, by the side of which was a clay jar that had been placed there with the body, and had contained either food or water.

The bodies had been in the ground so long, that most of the bones had crumbled to dust, and the remains could be distinguished from the white sand only by the gray, ashy color. Most of the pottery had likewise crumbled.

While digging in this old monument of a bygone age and race, I was reminded of the fact that dust and ashes is all that will, in a few years, remain of this daily-dying tenement of the soul. How little we realize the truth of this, surrounded as we are, by the vanities and cares of life, yet how important that it should have our foremost contemplation.

I reached Fernandina, Florida, on the seventh of January, 1879, and accepted a situation in one of the printing-offices, where I remained till the last of March, when I returned to the North.

From my place at the type-case or press, I could

see from the open office-windows, the orange-trees
full of fruit, the roses in gorgeous bloom, and the
little, barefooted boys and girls playing upon the
green lawns, and all this, too, while the Northern
States were white with snow and ice.

Fernandina contains a population of about three
thousand, and is situated on the Amelia River, two
miles from the Atlantic. The streets are wide and
well shaded with fine live-oak trees. Delightful and
balmy as the days are, the evenings are no less enchanting, and an evening walk upon the Shell-road
leading to the ocean, a stroll upon the Old Town
Board-walk, or out to the Draw-bridge, was a very
pleasant recreation after the duties of the day.

Fernandina is one of the most attractive places
in the state to test the allurements of the Floridan
winter. What is called winter, is only so in name,
in all other respects it is bright, glorious, blooming
June, with all the accompaniments of singing birds,
blooming flowers and sapphire skies.

It does a fair shipping trade in fruits, vegetables,
palmetto-goods and lumber. and ocean steamships
run from this port to New York and England.

The doors and windows are kept open half the
time, while fur-caps and overcoats are a curiosity.
Crops can be planted and gathered at all seasons of
the year, and many children are always barefooted.

Two miles from Fernandina is one of the finest
ocean beaches on the Atlantic Coast, and it is much

frequented for drives and promenades. It is ever lined with beautiful shells, thousands of which are carried to far-away Northern homes as relics.

In Florida, as well as in Georgia, South Carolina and the Gulf States, the palm, or palmetto-tree and plant, are found in great abundance. The leaf consists of thin, branching blades resembling daggers. The tree, which is sometimes known as the cabbage-palmetto, is from twenty to one hundred feet high, and the plant, or saw-palmetto, is from two to six feet in height.

The bud of the palm-tree is boiled and eaten by some people, and it is said to taste very much like boiled cabbage. There is no difference between the leaves of the tree and plant, other than that those of the tree are much the larger. The young leaves of the plant are used for making hats, fans, paper, baskets, mats, etc.

The leaf of the palm-tree is about a yard long, and two feet wide, while the stem of the leaf, which sprouts directly from the trunk, (the tree is without limbs,) is from four to six feet in length. During a shower of rain, the shelter of a palm-tree is almost as good as that of a roof.

The palm-tree of the South is supposed to be of the same kind as that mentioned in the Bible. The devout Roman Catholics of both the North and the South, obtain Florida palm-leaves for the purpose of decorating their cathedrals.

The roofs of houses, and houses entire, are made
of palm-leaves in Florida. I once visited a house
of this kind, near Fernandina, joined by some kind
friends who desired to show me a palmetto-home.
We found the inmates, an intelligent family, living
in great convenience. In one room a Dutch-oven,
containing a fire, served as a stove, and in another
apartment a heap of earth, upon which was a fire,
answered the same purpose. Both fires, I believe,
were used while cooking.

No inconvenience from smoke was experienced,
as it immediately went through the palmetto-roof.
This was evident from the fact that a fine old hen
was comfortably nestled upon a bed in one of the
rooms, where she was accustomed to lay her egg,
regardless of her surroundings.

The forests of Florida are beautiful and inviting.
The ground is covered with Nature's carpet of variegated colors—wild flowers and blossoms of the
most beautiful hues, and in great variety.

Florida, like Texas, is the home of the mammoth
cactus. Here are to be found many different kinds,
some of them growing to a height of from four to
twelve feet. The century-plant and other tropical
flowers also flourish here.

Orange culture is the principal occupation of the
Floridan planters. An orange-grove has somewhat
the appearance of a Northern peach-orchard. The
orange-tree does not bear until it becomes seven or

eight years old. A full-grown tree produces from five hundred to a thousand, and even fifteen hundred oranges. In Orange County, Florida, are vast forests of wild orange-trees, but as they, of course, were never grafted, the fruit, though abundant, is very sour, and unfit for eating. Native trees bear sweet oranges only after having been grafted with a scion of the Italian orange-tree.

Almost every person who owns a strip of ground, though it be no more than a small spot in front of their house, have one or more orange-trees. It is no unusual sight to see trees, full of fruit, surrounding the little negro cabins.

In addition to oranges, are grown bananas, figs, lemons, pine-apples, limes, sugar-cane, cotton, rice and other tropical products.

While at Fernandina I formed the acquaintance of an old Gulf ship captain and his family, living a few miles from town. They were the dearest, best friends I ever met among strangers, and the many pleasant times I spent with them, I will not forget.

The Captain, a hale, good-natured gentleman, had served in the Confederate Army, and had been confined in the North as a prisoner. When peace was restored, he commanded his own ship, a passenger craft, from St. Marks to Appalachicola, on the Gulf of Mexico. Becoming tired of sea-faring life, as all the "old salts" finally do, he "furled his sails and cast anchor on land."

The river and salt-water bayous, near his home, abounded with fish, oysters and clams, and we had some fine boat excursions after this kind of game, the affair generally ending with an oyster-supper, or an out-door oyster-roast, at the home of my friend, where the presence of his wife and family added to the pleasure of the occasion.

An oyster-bed is a curious and interesting sight. At low tide, the bars upon which the oysters grow, are entirely out of water, when the oysters can be gathered by going to the bars in a boat. Many of the bars are so thickly covered that it is impossible to walk upon them without stepping upon oysters.

Oysters always grow with their mouth upward, and they are often found in bunches, and upon old drift-wood, rocks, etc. The clusters growing upon bars somewhat resemble, in shape and position, a tract of dwarf cactus.

These beds, of course, vary in size, some of them are not more than ten or twenty feet in circumference, while others contain many acres. Oysters are public property about Fernandina, and they are so abundant that any person can obtain all they desire merely for the trouble of gathering them.

One day, while engaged in the monotonous duty of feeding a printing-press, I was handed an invitation to attend a candy-pulling, to be held at the residence of one of the citizens of Fernandina. I found some of the visitors already assembled when

I arrived, and soon the ceremony began. After the candy had been boiled, it was placed upon plates to cool. Each one of the ladies then took some of it in her hands and proceeded to the parlor.

Never having been at a candy-pulling before, and not knowing just what was expected of me, I was rather perplexed. However, a bright little damsel, perhaps divining my thoughts, came to my rescue, and giving me one end of her candy, said: "Now we will pull this until it becomes light."

So we pulled and pulled, exchanging ends again and again, while her chatty tongue kept ample pace with her nimble fingers. Finally, she declared that it looked "ever so nice," and then giving me half of the candy, we proceeded to test its merits.

The vicinity of Fernandina was once the favorite resort of the Georgia and North Florida Indians, who went there for the purpose of obtaining fish, oysters and clams. In some places, near the city, there are tracts of land so thickly covered with old oyster-shells—the relics of Indian feasts—that the ground is unfit for cultivation.

Here I found some ancient Indian pottery that had been used at oyster-feasts. Accompanied with that which I had obtained in a mound, previously mentioned in this chapter, I shipped it to the late Professor Haldeman.

In the suburb of Fernandina, towering above the dwellings like a grand monarchical pyramid of the

American aborigines, stands a vast Indian mound, the largest, perhaps, in the United States. Some relics, I believe, have been found in it, but an extended exploration of the mound was never made.

The colored folks throughout the South are very gracious to the whites, and I truly believe that the average Southern man and woman have ever been, and are still, about the best friends the blacks ever had. This is a broad assertion for a Northerner to make, still, I am not a Rebel, and would not buy or sell flesh and blood that encased a soul.

It has often been a question in my mind whether many of these good old black men and women will not find a seat in the Kingdom, while some of the stiff-necked, lordly white people will be compelled to occupy a locality not to be desired by their once meek and lowly servants.

I am not one of the white men who believe that the colored people are the descendants of a certain species of the brute creation, or that they have no soul, and less brains than a dog. Ignorant, little-souled white people may ill-treat and despise this poor, oppressed race, but if they ever become so fortunate as to "walk the streets of the City," they will be surprised to find black people there.

On Sunday evening, March 23, prior to my departure from Florida, I attended church with some friends, and as we walked along the streets, the air was laden with the sweet fragrance of the orange blossoms from hundreds of trees that bloomed at almost every dwelling.

During my travels and sojourns, I made some dear friends and many pleasant acquaintances, all of whom I will ever remember with love and kindness, though our future life and interest may drift far apart.

This is a world of partings, and the sooner this fact is realized, the better it will be for us, as we will then be more able to bear the pain.

True friendship! What a vast depth of love and beauty is comprised in this one sentence; yet how barren and meaningless it is when uttered by the cold, hollow voice of the world! We find but few, very few, real, sincere, unselfish friends. To find a kindred being with a heart warm, tender and true, is a boon I appreciate more than any other. The value of a true friend, one that understands us, and one with whom we can have free and harmonious interchange of thought, is far more desirable than all other worldly possessions.

Hazlitt once said that he desired but one thing to make him happy, and that was a true friend, and at another time he declared that, his heart shut up in its prison-house of clay, had never met a kindred heart to commune with.

CHAPTER XIX.

A land of lovely lakes that gem
    Her pleasant surface o'er and o'er;
A land of prairies broad and vast
    Like seas that never knew a shore.

A land where mighty rivers rise,
    Where stately pine trees proudly grow,
Where pleasant brooks forever run,
    And Minnehaha's waters flow.

THOS. L. SMITH.

FAREWELL TO FLORIDA—A VOYAGE ON THE ATLANTIC OCEAN—
TRENTON, CAMDEN AND WILMINGTON—FROM FLOWER-BEDS
TO SNOW-BANKS—ALTOONA, PITTSBURGH, FORT WAYNE AND
DUBUQUE—SCENERY ALONG THE UPPER MISSISSIPPI RIVER—
ST. PAUL—CARVER'S CAVE—FORT SNELLING—THE FALLS OF
MINNEHAHA—MINNEAPOLIS—THE FALLS OF ST. ANTHONY—
"THE FATHER OF WATERS"—FORT RIPLEY—A CHIPPEWA IS
KILLED BY HIS TRIBE FOR MARRYING A WHITE WOMAN—
AN INDIAN FALLS ASLEEP WITH A PIPE IN HIS MOUTH—
THE ST. LOUIS RIVER—DULUTH—VESSELS ICE-BOUND IN THE
GREAT LAKE IN THE MONTH OF MAY—A SAILING VOYAGE
ON LAKE SUPERIOR—BAYFIELD—MILWAUKEE.

GETTING aboard the steamer *Bridgeton*, I started for the North, going from Fernandina to Savannah by way of the Inside Route. Between these ports are vast ocean-inlets, or salt-water bayous, through which, at times, the steamer passed with difficulty, owing to the ebb of the tide. The scenery on the route is wild and tropical, and in some places, the shores are lined with groves of palm-trees.

At Savannah I sailed for New York in the fine steamship *Gate City,* and arrived in that port after a comparatively smooth voyage of fifty hours, still, I did not escape the spell of sea-sickness which, in most all cases, falls to the lot of a person unaccustomed to the rocking, plunging motion of a vessel at sea.

I made the voyage in this handsome iron craft through the courtesy of Captain Dagget, the commander, a quiet, unassuming man, who has grown gray on the ocean-wave. The sailors informed me that the sea was calm for the season, but at times, the waves rolled to a height of fifteen and twenty feet, and the huge steamer tossed and lurched like a great, living monster battling to escape from the angry, lashing billows.

Shortly after reaching New York, I went over to Philadelphia, by way of Newark and Trenton, and then proceeded on to Marietta, Pennsylvania, the home of my childhood.

Trenton, the capital of New Jersey, is situated on the Delaware, at the head of steamboat navigation, thirty miles above Philadelphia. It contains a population of thirty thousand.

Camden, New Jersey, opposite Philadelphia, is a handsome city, and the residence of many persons whose place of business is in Philadelphia. It is a great thoroughfare, during the summer, for travel to and from Cape May and Atlantic City. Its population is estimated to be about thirty thousand.

On the Delaware, thirty miles below Camden, is Wilmington, the largest town in Delaware. It is a thriving, wealthy place, containing forty thousand people. The city is engaged in the manufacture of railroad passenger-cars, steamboats, woolen goods, gunpowder and machinery.

I reached home on the first of April, and experienced some cold weather and several snow-storms during the month, which I keenly felt, and which were a marked contrast to the sunshine, fruit and flowers, that I had just left.

One bright, sunny morning in the latter part of the following May, I left for the West. Starting from the quiet, old village of Marietta, almost overshadowed by the sentinel-like Round Top and the Chickies Rock, from whose commanding summits can be seen the most enchanting rural scenes in the country, I, in due time, reached Altoona, and then proceeded across the mountains to Pittsburgh.

. Altoona, situated near the foot of the Alleghany Mountains, is a very stirring, energetic city. It is emphatically a railroad town, and contains the car-shops and locomotive-factory of the Pennsylvania Railroad. The population is sixteen thousand.

Pittsburgh, located at the junction of the Alleghany and Monongahela Rivers, is the largest coal and iron mart in America, and is surrounded with numerous and extensive mines of both materials.

The furnaces, rolling-mills and other works, are so numerous that the smoke from their chimneys ever hangs over the city like a black, threatening cloud. A large river trade is done with the Southern and Western cities, by steamboats. Pittsburgh contains about one hundred and twenty thousand people.

Fort Wayne, one of the most important cities in Indiana, is a prominent railroad center, and is also largely engaged in manufacturing machinery, etc.

Continuing westward, I reached St. Paul, going through Chicago, Clinton, Dubuque and Northfield.

Dubuque, lying upon high bluffs overlooking the Mississippi River and the surrounding country for miles, is an attractive town. Considerable trade is carried on with the different river ports. Lead in large quantities is mined near Dubuque. The city claims a population of twenty-six thousand.

The Mississippi, between Clinton and Prairie du-Chien, and further up, is very similar in its general character and surroundings, to the Missouri and its adjacent country between Omaha and Sioux City, and that further north.

The bluffs along the Mississippi, between these points, are high and rugged. In some places, they are covered with fine groves of cottonwood, maple, birch, butternut and plum trees, in other localities, they are entirely destitute of timber.

These hills consist of sandstone and limestone and their bare and broken sides, as they approach the water, present objects of interest. It requires no great stretch of the imagination to fancy these objects to be the ruins of temple, castle and spire.

From St. Anthony's Falls to the Upper Rapids, near Davenport, a distance of three hundred miles, the Mississippi, during severe winters, is a safe and unbroken thoroughfare for travel by sleighs. The farmers frequently transport their crops to market by this mode of river navigation.

At Northfield, Minnesota, I had the pleasure of meeting Mr. Thos. L. Smith, the printer-poet. He is a gentleman of kindly heart and genial manners, and has won a host of friends and admirers by the grace and beauty of his poems. The verses which head chapters five and nineteen of this work, were written expressly for it by Mr. Smith.

St. Paul is situated on the Mississippi, near the head of steamboat navigation, and nearly twenty-one hundred miles from its mouth. A Frenchman, named Pierre Parrant, was the first white man who located on the ground now occupied by St. Paul. He built the first log house here in 1838, and then began to trade with the Indians.

Although Parrant was the first to locate, he had not been the first to visit the spot. In 1680 Father Louis Hennepin, a Jesuit missionary, visited this place while being held in captivity by the Indians, and in 1766 Captain Jonathan Carver, held a grand council with the Sioux in a large cave which bears his name, and which is located half a mile from the city steamboat landing.

St. Paul does a very large trade with the states and territories of the Northwest. It is handsomely situated upon three plateaux of land, and is partly encircled by a ridge of timber-crowned bluffs, that rise grandly above their surroundings. The population is fifty thousand. In the suburbs are many costly and beautiful private residences, and most elegantly-arranged grounds.

The natural scenery near St. Paul is enchanting, and that beheld from the river bridge, or Summit Avenue, is sublime. The winding stream, rugged bluffs, sloping mounds, and the grand Minnesota Valley beyond, are sights to call forth admiration.

While in St. Paul, I was engaged in setting type on the *History of St. Paul*, a graphic and elegantly illustrated account of the city's past and present, published by T. M. Newson, the pioneer publisher of the city, whose books and magazine, the *Fireside Companion*, are models of typographical beauty and literary merit.

Carver's Cave is located at the foot of a bluff, on the east bank of the Mississippi. Its entrance is about nine feet wide and five feet high. Entering the first room, an arena-like cavity about fifteen feet high and thirty feet wide, the floor, sides and roof, are found to consist of soft, white sandstone.

A short distance from the mouth of the cavern a

beautiful little lake begins, and extends beyond the scope of vision. Its water is very calm, clear and cool, and has no visible feeder. Various smaller chambers branch off from the main cave.

About two miles further up the river is another cave. It is similar in appearance to Carver's, but a running stream is found in it instead of a lake.

Five miles above St. Paul, at the junction of the Mississippi and Minnesota, is Fort Snelling, about the oldest military post in the Northwest, having been erected in 1820. It is now used as a supply post for other forts and Indian agencies further in the interior. It stands upon the summit of a large white sandstone bluff, seventy feet above the banks of the two rivers which wind around its base, and commands a fine view of the surrounding country for many miles.

The beautiful and romantic Falls of Minnehaha are situated about midway between Fort Snelling and Minneapolis, and are much visited by tourists from the East and South. Minnehaha has a beauty and grandeur peculiar to itself, which consists not in depth of water or ruggedness of precipice. The traveler, not acquainted with the exact location of Minnehaha, could pass within two hundred yards of it without being aware of his nearness to it, so quiet and secluded is the beautiful cascade.

At high water, the falls are not more than sixty feet wide, and the water, before it reaches the pre-

cipice, is only a small, calm-flowing brook. But, all
at once, the modest little creek widens in its narrow
bed, and then reaching a flat sandstone rock, leaps
over its brink, and falling upon a bench of smaller
rocks below, forms the sparkling and ever-musical
Falls of Minnehaha.

The water dashes over the precipice in one even
and unbroken sheet, which is a singular and pretty
feature of the cascade.   Behind the falls is a grand
promenade beneath an arch, which, although made
by the moulding hand of Nature, has the aspect of
having been carved out by man.   Here the visitor
can walk or sit without inconvenience from dashing
spray, while the sheet of water leaps directly over
his head into the dark, narrow ravine below.

Minnehaha was formerly a favorite resort of the
Sioux Indians, from whom it received its present
name, which means, "Laughing Water."

Minneapolis, situated on the Mississippi, at the
Falls of St. Anthony, and ten miles above St. Paul,
is one of the handsomest cities in the West.   It is
very energetic and flourishing, and contains about
fifty thousand people.

The country, for miles about the city, consists of
beautiful prairie land.   Business houses of grand
proportions, and of fine architecture, are seen upon
all of the principal streets, while the mansions and
cottages, and the pretty grounds that environ them,
have a rural attractiveness that is most enchanting

after leaving the din and bustle of the commercial section of the city.

A very pleasing feature of Minneapolis homes is the beautiful front yards, which have been banked up with ground several feet above the level of the streets, and are without any fence, while they form lovely green plateaux, pleasantly interspersed with fountains, statues and flowers.

The city is extensively engaged in manufacturing flour, lumber and woolen goods. Several bridges span the Mississippi at this point, from which can be had a grand view of the Falls of St. Anthony.

The falls are a great natural wonder. The river here has a perpendicular fall of eighteen feet, and the effect is very imposing. The water-power which the falls furnish is very valuable, and is, probably, the strongest and most available in the country.

The Falls of St. Anthony were discovered in the year 1680, by Father Louis Hennepin, the Jesuit missionary, who gave them the name they bear.

The river at Minneapolis, and for several miles below the town, is rapid, and flows between high, steep bluffs, which, during the summer, are clothed in Nature's mantle of green, pleasantly dotted with groves of butternut, oak and plum trees.

Leaving Minneapolis, I continued northward to Brainerd, and from that place I proceeded over to Duluth, on the head of Lake Superior. Between Minneapolis and Brainerd the Mississippi is a very

modest little stream, but it is quite valuable for the
purpose of floating logs to the Minneapolis mills.
The country along its banks consists of prairie, interspersed with small groves of dwarf oak.

A few miles above the Falls of St. Anthony, the
rugged sandstone bluffs, which predominate for a
distance of five hundred miles below the falls, are
no longer seen, and the river banks are lower and
more sloping.

The Mississippi—"the father of waters"—is one
of the wonders of America. Having Itasca Lake
for its fountain head, or source, about thirty miles
north of Brainerd, by land, it traverses a section of
country thirteen hundred miles in extent, although
the river, owing to its winding course, is twenty-five
hundred miles in length.

After rising in a land where winter lingers long,
it sweeps through various shades of climate, finally
losing itself in the great Gulf of Mexico, upon the
shores of which summer perpetually exists.

About eighteen miles south of Brainerd, close to
the river's edge, is Fort Ripley. Near this place
the renowned Chippewa chieftain, Hole-in-the-Day,
was cruelly murdered by his own tribe because he
had married a white woman in Washington.

This Indian once held a council with the Sioux,
and several military men and their wives went to
see the ceremony. At this the Sioux became very
angry, and left, saying to Hole-in-the-Day that if

he wanted to hold a council with "white squaws,"
he should do it alone.

This did not displease the Chippewa leader, and
shaking each of the ladies cordially by the hand,
he said:

"I am happy to see so many sweet women here
with their winning smiles, and they are all welcome
to a seat on my side of the council." ·

While walking through the forest near Brainerd
one morning, I noticed two Chippewa Indians lying
upon the ground a short distance in front of me:
and upon going up to them, I found that they were
sound asleep.

Having the appearance of being intoxicated, they
must have started from town for their camp, on the
previous night, but having drank too freely from a
suspicious-looking flask which they had with them.
they had become unable to reach their village, and
and had dropped down in a drunken sleep, where I
found them.

One of the Indians had fallen asleep with a pipe
in his mouth, where it still remained, while the rum-
clouded mind of the savage was in the supposed
"land of dreams."

The country between Brainerd and Duluth contains vast tracts of land producing raspberries in
great abundance, and of a fine quality. During the
season, the Indians subsist chiefly upon this fruit.
prepared with maple-sugar of their own make.

About thirty miles west of Duluth the country becomes hilly, and great heaps of jagged, broken rocks are on every hand, while the vast pine forests add a strangely wild grandeur to the scenery.

The St. Louis River, flowing into Lake Superior, is a very dark and boisterous stream. Its bed and shores, in some places, are almost one entire mass of rocks, and it is ever rushing and surging on its course to the great inland sea.

Duluth is located upon a high, rocky bluff, facing the head of Lake Superior, the mirror-like surface of which, during a calm, reflects the town and its surroundings vividly. While there is nothing very attractive about the town, the lake forms an object of beauty and interest.

The winters are long and severe, but the people prepare themselves for a siege of snow and ice, and are attached to their Northern home. They speak in glowing terms of the fine sleighing, coasting and skating, they enjoy during the winter.

During my sojourn in the town, in the month of August, the weather was cool and Autumnal, and in the morning and evening, the tourists from the South donned their overcoats. The population of Duluth is about five thousand.

The water of Lake Superior is cold even in the summer, and it is used by the citizens of Duluth instead of well water. I was told that on July 4, 1875, some of the Duluth people obtained ice from among the rocks, along the lake shore, for making ice-cream; and in May of the same year, seventeen vessels were ice-bound near Duluth.

Lines of iron steamships ply between this port and Milwaukee, Chicago, Detroit, Cleveland, Erie and Buffalo, and thousands of sailing vessels are constantly, during the navigable season, ploughing through this and neighboring lakes, carrying their cargoes of wheat, lumber, copper-ore, etc.

One fine morning, in the latter part of August, I stepped aboard the schooner *Emma*, bound across the lake from Duluth to Bayfield, Wisconsin, one hundred and three miles distant. The vessel was in charge of Captain Fred. Herbert, and C. Leihy, the mate, both of Bayfield. These gentlemen have been sailing upon the Great Lakes since boyhood, and are thorough navigators.

We left port with a light breeze, which increased as we receded from the shore, and in a little while, we were in "the swell" of the mighty lake. In our rear was the highland city, and the rocky, pine-clad North Shore, while directly in front of us, was the vast expanse of rolling billows.

Lake Superior is four hundred and thirty miles long, and at the widest place, it is one hundred and thirty miles from shore to shore, while its principal depth is nine hundred feet. The water is so clear that objects can be seen at a distance of twenty or thirty feet from the surface, and when the water is calm, it reflects objects as clearly as a mirror does.

The scenery on its shores is rather monotonous, consisting, mostly, of rugged, timber-covered hills. There are, as yet, no towns or settlements along the lake shore between Duluth and Bayfield, with the exception of one lighthouse and an Indian agency.

Never having traveled in a sailing vessel before, I enjoyed the trip very much, and passed the time in sauntering about the ship with the sailors, climbing through the rigging, shooting at gulls from the cross-trees on the masts, and otherwise making the best of the voyage.

Captain Herbert was thoroughly acquainted with the "ways of the world," and well knowing that a newspaper man always expects free passage, and to be feasted, petted and have his questions answered, as an equivalent for the "notice" he is expected to write, this good-natured captain, after we had left port, addressed me about as follows:

"Well, Mr. Editor, once again we are at sea, now, the whole range of the craft, and all the crew, are at your kind disposal; make the best of us and the accommodations, but don't publish to the world the fact that sailors are the worst of humanity."

On reaching Bayfield, I accompanied him home to tea, for he was eager to have me see his "pretty little wife." I was very hospitably entertained by Mrs. Herbert, and found her to be a lady of education and refinement, and one of those deep, quiet little women whom it is a pleasure to meet in these days, when gaudy attire, loose, shallow conversation and an affected demeanor, characterize so many of the fair sex.

Bayfield is a popular summer resort, and is very finely situated on the northern coast of Wisconsin. Being surrounded by the Apostle Islands, it is one of the best sheltered ports on Lake Superior. It is quite an attractive town, the houses are neat and cozy, and handsome maple shade trees and sparkling fountains adorn the streets.

The day following our arrival, Captain Herbert set sail and conveyed me over to Ashland, sixteen miles distant. Here I took the Wisconsin Central Railroad for Milwaukee, and from that city I went to Chicago on the steamer *Sheboygan*, through the kindness of Mr. Clark, the gentlemanly purser.

Between Ashland and Stevens Point, a distance of about two hundred miles, the railroad traverses an immense, and almost unbroken pine forest, the only inhabitants, beside a few bands of Chippewas, being the railroad hands and some lumbermen.

Milwaukee is a handsome and wealthy city, and is finely situated on Lake Michigan, eighty miles north of Chicago. Its population is one hundred and twenty thousand, and the lake trade is large.

Reaching Chicago, I obtained a pass to my home from the officers of the Pittsburgh, Fort Wayne & Chicago Railway, arriving in September, 1879.

CHAPTER XX.

Oh! carry me back to Tennessee,
There let me live and die;
Among the fields of yellow corn,
Where my old parents lie.

ANON.

In February following, I went to Tennessee and Kentucky, for the purpose of exploring the ancient Indian camp-grounds, and the caves of these two states, in quest of Indian relics for the lamented Professor Haldeman.

Reaching Baltimore, I embarked for Norfolk in the steamship *Resolute*, commanded by Captain C. Nelson, who very kindly tendered me the privilege of his vessel, pointed out objects of interest along the route, and did much to make the trip pleasant.

Steaming away from the busy docks, and out of the harbor, we were soon ploughing through the briny waves of Chesapeake Bay. As the weather was stormy, the waves were high, and the steamer rocked and plunged considerably, and I experienced a spell of sea-sickness that reminded me of my voyage from Savannah to New York.

Passing Hampton Roads and Fortress Monroe, we entered the harbor of Norfolk. Here we found at anchor, the United States men-of-war, *Tennessee* and *Powhatan.*

At Baltimore the ground was covered with snow, but upon reaching Norfolk, about one hundred and eighty miles further south, no snow or ice could be seen; the weather was mild and balmy, while the grass was green, and the early vegetables already above the surface. The change was as pleasant as it was sudden.

Norfolk is situated on Elizabeth River, thirty-two miles from the Atlantic Ocean, and opposite Portsmouth. Its harbor is excellent, and admits vessels of the largest size. There are vast oyster-beds near the city, and the oyster trade is a leading industry.

Norfolk is a genuine Southern city, and a person from the North has no difficulty in seeing that he is in a city, and among people widely different from those he has been used to. But he can hardly be displeased, for the town has attractions peculiar to itself, and the people are friendly and courteous.

Portsmouth is connected with Norfolk by a ferry, and it is a handsome little city, containing thirteen thousand people, which is a little more than half of the number contained in Norfolk. Some railroad-shops, manufactories and a navy-yard, are located at Portsmouth.

The country people near these two cities are engaged in growing early vegetables for Baltimore, Philadelphia and New York markets. The colored people are numerous, and perform nearly all of the field labor.

From Norfolk I proceeded to Lynchburg. The country between these places is rather level, and is largely interspersed with vast pine forests, but on nearing the latter town, the surface becomes hilly, and the land is more productive and much better cultivated than the section lying between Norfolk and Burkeville.

In the pine districts, wood can often be obtained for the labor of cutting it. Stoves are seldom used in the country, and the old-fashioned fireplaces are still popular. Lamps are often dispensed with, for the blazing fire of resinous pine forms a light by which a person can easily sew or read. The people in Southern Virginia suffered considerably during the war, from the devastation of both armies, and they have not yet fully recovered from the blight.

Between Lynchburg and Bristol, the country is mountainous, the Blue Ridge and Alleghany Moun-

tains extending entirely across the western part of
the state.   In many places are found very excellent
agricultural and stock-raising localities, and much
better farms and buildings are seen here than in.
the more eastern sections of Virginia.

There are many fine valleys in this district, and
some localities reminded me of old Pennsylvania.
Especially was this the case in the vicinity of the
Peaks of Otter and Big Lick; here are settlements
of "Pennsylvania Germans," a class of people who
surround themselves with "peace and plenty," no
matter where they are.

Reaching Bristol, I proceeded to Knoxville, and
after searching for Indian relics along the Holston
River, I went to Chattanooga and Nashville, thence
to Cincinnati, going by way of the Mammoth Cave
and Louisville, continuing my hunts for antiquities
at various points along the way.

Tennessee and Kentucky were once the favorite
resorts of the Indians, as the implements of war
and domestic use that are still found, amply prove.
Near Knoxville and Chattanooga, in Tennessee, and
in the vicinity of Bowling Green, Mammoth Cave
and Elizabethtown, in Kentucky, remain traces of
vast arrow-head factories.   The ground is strewn
with flint chips, and arrow-heads in various stages
of completion, from the rough flint rock to the perfect arrow-head.

A few miles from Knoxville I found evidences of

an ancient Indian camp, and arrow-heads and frag-
ments of pottery still lay upon the surface. Near
the Mammoth Cave, and at the entrance of Indian
Cave, in Kentucky, I found some fine spear-heads,
arrow-heads, flint-knives, etc.

Nashville, the capital of Tennessee, is a neat and
attractive city, and is situated on the Cumberland
River, about two hundred miles from its confluence
with the Ohio. It contains thirty thousand people,
and is a prominent railroad and commercial center.

The dwellings are neither grand nor showy, for
the majority of them are neat little cottages, most
enchantingly environed by beautiful lawns, flower-
beds and orchards. The city's principal feature of
beauty is its neat, cozy, rural-appearing homes.

At Nashville is located the printing, stereotyping
and publishing house of the Methodist Episcopal
Church, South, and many of its publications equal
any issued from Northern cities, in regard to their
typographical beauty and general workmanship.

The country about Nashville is the richest in the
state. Here are found turnpike-roads, crops, farms
and houses, that remind a "Yankee" of home. On
the road leading from Nashville to Gallatin, are to
be seen some farms and buildings quite as fine as
the average of those found in Pennsylvania, Ohio
and Indiana. · But since the war, both the land and
the buildings have been sadly neglected, and now
present a somewhat deserted and run down aspect,

compared with what they were previous to the war.

The extensive plantations, the groups of merry black folks, the planters' grand mansions, in which wealth, luxury and hospitality abounded, are now far from being what they once were.

From Nashville I went up to Bowling Green, in Kentucky. This is a town of five thousand people, and is surrounded by grand, timber-clad hills, that stretch away in every direction as far as the eye can reach. Leaving this town, I proceeded to Glasgow Junction, where I left the railroad and went over to see the world-renowned Mammoth Cave, seven or eight miles distant, through a dense forest.

. At the Cave Hotel I met Mr. W. S. Miller, the gentlemanly lessee and manager of the hotel and cave, who kindly furnished me William, one of the cave guides, some lamps, and all the necessary accompaniments for a stroll through this marvelous underground world of wonders.

Although a man might travel in every country on the globe, and see every thing that could interest a traveler, except this cave, the greatest curiosity of all would yet remain to be seen.

I spent half a day in the cave with an intelligent guide, and walked through its rooms and avenues for a distance of nine miles, still, I am not competent to give the reader a proper description of its awful sublimity, its amazing attractions.

The Mammoth Cave is situated in the southwest-

ern section of Kentucky, ninety-five miles south of
Louisville, and seven or eight miles from the Louisville & Nashville Railroad. The mouth of the cave
is reached by a deep, rocky ravine, and the entrance
to it is twenty-five feet high and thirty feet wide.

The cave was undoubtedly formed by the action
of water and chemical agencies. The substances of
which the top, sides and floor, of the cave consist,
are generally limestone, gypsum, sulphate of soda,
alabaster and nitrate of lime, all of which, I believe,
bear a close chemical relation.

This cavern consists not of one or a few cavities,
for it contains nearly two hundred rooms, avenues,
arenas, tunnels and pits, leading off into different
directions, and connecting with others that have, as
yet, not been fully explored.

It is said that there are hundreds of rooms and
pits that have never been entered; the total length
of those thoroughly known by the guides is about
one hundred miles. This, it should be understood,
is the united length of all the explored apartments.
Its main length, as far as known, is ten miles.

Many of these chambers have been beautifully
and symmetrically formed by Nature, though it is
difficult to dispel the idea that it was not done by
the hands of expert, untiring workmen—by a race
of men long since extinct, yet leaving behind them
a monument of their art. Some of the rooms are
circular in form, while the ceilings are as perfectly

in unison with the general feature of the rooms, as though they had been carved out of solid rock by the sculptor's handicraft.

The contents of these rooms consist of curiously shaped rocks, and combinations of limestone and gypsum, which by some singular agency, have been wrought into almost every conceivable form, and in the terribly silent gloom of this tomb-like place, a visitor is filled with feelings of awe and solemnity that baffle description.

The sides, floors and ceilings, in some places, are covered with crystals of gypsum and carbonate of lime of great brilliancy and beauty, while the top seems to be supported by immense stalactites and stalagmites, which are as symmetrical in form as the pillars that support a grand portico.

All the imaginary cave-retreats of highwaymen, that novelists love to describe, sink into insignificance when compared with this, regarding beauty and resemblance to the work of human hands. In some rooms, the floor is quite level, and consists of sand and gravel; in others the way is obstructed by huge heaps of rock, yet on the sides or ceiling, are no traces of the rock having fallen down.

The dripping of water mingled with chemicals—principally sulphate of soda, gypsum, alabaster and saltpetre, together with oxide of iron, has become solidified, and formed huge and almost transparent pillars, which reach from floor to ceiling. They are to be seen in all stages of formation, from the time they first crop out, until they reach from ceiling to floor. In addition to these, there are various other crystallizations and petrifactions, which somewhat resemble human forms, animals, birds, trees, stars, flowers, fruit, snow, icicles, etc., etc.

There are much larger objects which have been formed by the same slow, dripping process, such as huge arches, grottoes, spires, tables, bridges, etc. Many of these are studded with crystals which, in the bright glare of the lamps, present scenes of the most grotesque and dazzling beauty.

The cave contains some fine springs of ice-cold water, which near the surface, is pure and pleasant to the taste, but near the bottom it is very strongly impregnated with sulphur. One of these springs, known to the guides as Lake Purity, is perfectly transparent, and had the guide not informed me of it, I would have walked right into it, for without a close examination, it was impossible, by the light of a lamp, to see that any water intervened between the gravelly bed that formed its bottom.

William, my guide, had been engaged in piloting tourists about in the Mammoth Cave for fourteen years, and he was the most intelligent and well-read colored man I ever met. He was versed in various works of history and travels, and in the literature of the times, and his knowledge of chemistry and geology would be a credit to men who make much

greater pretentions than this humble, plodding son
of Africa.

Thus it ever is, the hasty judgment and narrowmindedness of those shallow souls who can never
discover, beneath an unassuming, homely exterior,
qualities of heart and mind much superior to their
own, often contemptuously pass real worth without
knowing it, because their ignorance and pride ever
blinds them to the fact that brains and an honest
heart, is not, as a rule, heralded by a flashy attire
and a vaunting tongue.

In this subterranean world are lakes and rivers,
varying from one-fourth to three-fourths of a mile
in length, and from twenty to a hundred feet wide,
while their depth is from ten to thirty feet. Where
the water comes from, or where it goes to, is not
certainly known, though it is supposed to have an
undiscovered connection with Green River.

In these waters are found eyeless fish; they are
of a peculiar species, and do not deposit eggs like
other fish, but give birth to their young. They are
perfectly white, and from four to eight inches long.

Shortly after entering the cave, the Rotunda is
reached. This is an immense arena-like cavity, one
hundred feet high. Its floor is still covered with
the remains of vats, and wooden water-pipes which
were used by saltpetre miners in 1812–14. Silence
here reigns supreme, and a person can count the
pulsations of his own heart by listening to its beat,

so amazingly silent is this most wonderful cavern.
After leaving this place the visitor arrives at the
Methodist Church; it is eighty feet in diameter and
forty feet high. A cluster of rocks twenty-five feet
high, forms a pulpit, and a number of logs, which
served as benches, still remain as they were left by
people who worshipped there in the early part of
the present century.

Near the Methodist Church is the Bridal Stand,
consisting of two icicle-shaped pillars, which reach
from floor to ceiling. A pretty story of woman's
love and cunning is connected with it. A young
lady once promised her mother that she would not
marry the best man on top of the earth. At last,
however, she met her fate, but not wanting to displease her lover, or prove the vow to her mother to
be false, she artfully suggested to her betrothed a
plan of marriage in the Mammoth Cave. He very
cheerfully accepted her proposition, and while the
minister performed the ceremony, the conscientious
bride stood between the two beautiful stalagmites
which have since been known as the Bridal Stand.

After the wedding, the dutiful daughter returned
to her mother, and introducing her husband, gave
her mother to understand that, although she really
had the best man on top of the earth, she did not
marry him there.

The Star Chamber is an interesting feature. Its
ceiling consists of black gypsum, interspersed with

an occasional white spot formed by some freak of
Nature. When the guide partly conceals the lamps,
these white spots, on their dark background, most
vividly resemble the stars of the sky.

Some time ago the petrified bodies of an Indian
woman and a child were found in one of the pits.
They had probably wandered into the cave years
before the place was known to white men, and not
being able to find. their way out, had perished in
this mammoth tomb. My guide informed me that
he had found skulls, tomahawks, arrow-heads and
other traces of Indians, in the cave.

A person becoming lost in the cave, without any
hope of getting out, would probably perish from
mental agony. A visitor once wandered from his
party, when his light became extinguished, and in
this terrible plight—left alone in utter darkness, in
the horrible·gloom of that unearthly solitude, he
became a raving maniac.

In this condition he secreted himself behind a
huge rock, where he remained for two days and a
night before the guides found him. While hunting
him, they frequently passed his place of conceal-
ment, but he remained perfectly silent, and, when
by a mere accident, the guides discovered him, he
endeavored to get away from them.

One day a lady lingered so far behind her company that she could not hear their voices, and while
trying to overtake her friends, she fell, extinguish-

ing her light at the same moment. Terrified at her
situation, she became insensible, and when found
by the guides, her mind was deranged, and she remained insane for several years after.

The guides say that every year they are obliged
to go in search of visitors who foolishly wander off
from their party, and become utterly bewildered.
When found, they are generally crying or praying,
and, sometimes, insanity has already taken place.

It would be next to impossible for a person not
acquainted with the cavern, to find his way out, for
when once inside, a score of avenues, tunnels and
pits, lead off into every direction, and all of them
are so similar in form and general appearance, that
he would not know by which ones he had entered.

No mind can conceive, or pen fully portray, the
great sublimity, the wonderfully awe-inspiring influence, the manifold scenes of natural beauty, of
this silent, mammoth dungeon.

The Mammoth Cave is best reached by the way
of Cave City, a town on the Louisville & Nashville
Railroad. On the arrival of trains, a stage conveys
visitors to the cave, seven miles distant. The Cave
Hotel can accommodate two hundred guests, and it
is furnished in admirable style, while the table and
waiters are all that could be desired.

The country around the cave is wild and rugged,
consisting of a thickly-timbered mountain district.
The locality is as secluded and sparsely settled as

though it had not been a favorite resort for nearly
a hundred years. Within a short distance of the
hotel hunting, fishing and boating, can be enjoyed.

There are several smaller caverns in this vicinity,
which may be branches of the Mammoth Cave, but
a connection has not been found. They vary from
one hundred yards to a mile in length, and in their
general aspect, they resemble the Mammoth Cave.
The principal ones are, Horse Cave, White's Cave,
Dickison's Cave, Indian Cave and Grand Cave.

From Cave City I proceeded to Louisville. This
is a city of one hundred and sixty thousand people,
and is a wealthy, stirring place. It is a prominent
railroad and steamboat town, and a manufacturing
point of importance. Handsome river steamers ply
between Louisville and the Ohio, Mississippi and
Missouri River ports.

Leaving this place, I continued on to Cincinnati.
Indianapolis, one hundred and nine miles north of
Louisville, is the capital of Indiana, and one of the
greatest railroad centers in the world. The country
around the city consists of prairie, and it is fertile
and very valuable. The population of Indianapolis
is about one hundred and fifteen thousand.

Columbus, the capital of Ohio, is located on the
Scioto River, and is largely engaged in manufacturing iron, woolen and other goods. It contains over
fifty thousand inhabitants, and is surrounded by a
good agricultural district.

Cincinnati, one of the principal Western cities, is situated on the Ohio River, and does a large river trade with Pittsburgh, Louisville, St. Louis, Memphis, New Orleans and the Upper Mississippi and Missouri River countries. The city is partly environed by handsome, timber-clad hills, upon which are many grand and costly private residences. The place contains a population of about two hundred and twenty thousand, and in size and commercial importance, it ranks as the third city in the West.

Cincinnati is about the only city of its size in the country, from whose bustling docks can be seen the calm, peaceful country, and the quiet farm-houses. A short distance below Ludlow, on the Kentucky side of the river, and four or five miles from the principal business center of Cincinnati, can readily be seen the quiet country homes nestled along the base of the bluffs, which form a delightful contrast to the eyes weary of gazing upon the dust and ever smoke-begrimed city.

This city is connected with Covington and Newport, Kentucky, by a fine suspension bridge. The latter named places are thriving young cities, and are largely engaged in various iron manufacturies. The towns are surrounded, on the south, by timber-crowned bluffs, beyond which is the famous Blue Grass section of Central Kentucky.

From Cincinnati I started for home, going up to Pittsburgh on the steamer *Katie Stockdale*, through

the courtesy of Captain M. F. Noll, now commander of the fine new steamer *Scotia*, of Pittsburgh.
The Captain knew just how a traveling newspaper
man expects to be entertained, and much was done
to make the trip pleasant and enjoyable for me.

The natural scenery along the Upper Ohio is attractive, and there are many pretty towns and noisy
cities, as well as secluded farms, to be seen upon
its banks.

Captain Noll is yet a young man, but he is a very
popular and efficient steamboat man, well known at
every landing between Cincinnati and Pittsburgh
for his qualities as a captain and a true gentleman,
having been running on Ohio River steamers since
boyhood. He talks but little, is quiet and reserved,
yet courteous and respectful to all, and he has that
peculiar faculty of managing a steamboat and crew
without oaths or bluster.

There is an old saying to the effect that the table
of a steamboat is spread with the best in the land,
and I must say that the fare on this steamer was of
such quantity and quality, as to make the traveler
wish that steamboat fare would ever be his portion.

The distance from Cincinnati to Pittsburgh, by
river, is four hundred and sixty-six miles, and the
principal places along the route are Huntingdon,
Parkersburg and Wheeling. The latter city is the
capital of West Virginia, and contains a population
of thirty thousand. It is an extensive coal and iron

mart, and like Pittsburgh, it is constantly draped
in dense clouds of smoke and cinders which issue
from the many furnace and rolling-mill chimneys.

Soon after landing at Pittsburgh, I proceeded to
my home, where I arrived in April, 1880.

"Roughing it" on the plains, and in the forests
and mountains, in all kinds of weather, and among
all kinds of people, and suffering all the hardships,
fatigue, inconvenience and disappointments, which
fall to the lot of the hunter of antiquities, was not
always an agreeable task, but Professor Haldeman
was ever a prompt and liberal employer, and to his
kindness, generosity, and untiring zeal in collecting
the antiquities of the North American Indians, I am
indebted for many of my journeys. His influence
and letters always secured me favors and kindness
from the railroad and steamboat officials, as well as
from editors and others.

A few months after my return from the South,
this renowned scientist, linguist and author, died
very suddenly at his home at Chickies, Lancaster
County, Pennsylvania, aged sixty-eight years, leaving a most estimable wife, and two sons and two
daughters to mourn his loss.

Professor S. S. Haldeman was born in the year
1812, at Locust Grove Mills, Pennsylvania. Of an
agreeable and vivacious address, he had a host of
friends, and the admiration and honor of the scientific, educational and literary men, of both America

and Europe. He was the author of various standard scientific, educational and other works, and he contributed largely to the scientific and educational journals of the day.

Early in life he directed his attention to science, geology, conchology, ethnology, language and the antiquities of the Indians, in which he was an acknowledged authority; and his cabinets and libraries were among the best in existence.

He had traveled extensively on both Continents in the interest of his favorite branches of science; and he was versed in the Arabic, German, Hebrew, Latin, Greek, Welsh and other languages. A Philadelphia journalist asserts that the Professor was versed, to some extent, in every language that had a literature.

He was always kind, generous, and a substantial friend to all whom he deemed worthy of friendship such as few men, save himself, knew how to show.

Frank and genial, honored by all, the most zealous advocate of truth, research and science, stricken at the brink of "three score years and ten," yet in the very midst of a busy, useful life, we would humbly lay the "wreath of immortelles" upon thy honored grave!

CHAPTER XXI.

'Mid pleasures and palaces though we may roam,
Still, be it ever so humble, there's no place like home:
A charm from the skies seems to hallow it there,
Which, go through the world, you'll not meet with elsewhere.

Home, home, sweet home!
There's no place like home!

An exile from home, pleasure dazzles in vain:
Ah! give me my lowly thatch'd cottage again;
The birds singing sweetly, that came at my call—
Give me them, and that peace of mind dearer than all.

Home, home, sweet home!
There's no place like home!

J. HOWARD PAYNE.

I START FOR FLORIDA AGAIN, AND RESOLVE TO MAKE THIS MY
LAST TRIP—"THERE IS NO PLACE LIKE HOME"—A WRECK
WASHED ASHORE—THE VARIATIONS OF CLIMATE BETWEEN
FLORIDA AND THE NORTH—THE PAST AND PRESENT OF THE
CAPITAL CITY OF PENNSYLVANIA—A REVERIE—I AT LAST
SETTLE DOWN TO ROAM NO MORE—FOOD FOR THOUGHT.

IN the following winter I started for the South again, making Florida my destination. From Pennsylvania I proceeded to Morristown, Tennessee, by way of Harper's Ferry, Staunton and Bristol.

I had resolved to make this my last trip, intending upon my return, to locate and go into business, for I had become heartily tired of traveling, and longed for a more settled, secluded life.

Go where we may, "there is no place like home." The more we wander, the stronger this fact comes home to our hearts, and the older we get, the more we realize and appreciate the truth of the saying.

In dwelling upon this theme of home, I am reminded of a very excellent home book entitled, *The Complete Home*, by Mrs. Julia McNair Wright, who, perhaps, is the only woman in America that could write such a practical and entertaining encyclopædia of domestic matters, and at the same time so harmoniously infuse into its pages the best counsel, the cream of common sense, the brightest gems of refined and ennobling sentiments, and envelop the whole in the enchanting halo of a Christian tone.

The gifted authoress has put her soul, as well as her life experience, into this, her best work. The contents, while bearing upon every department of a complete home and its management, are characterized by a style that recognizes "Mother, Home and Heaven," as the three dearest words in language.

The book is issued by J. C. McCurdy & Co., of Philadelphia, publishers of standard works, whose imprint is enough to warrant for a book all that beautiful engravings, handsome paper, clear print and elegant binding can make it.

Reader, you probably think that this is a book-notice, and you are right, as the fair authoress and her publishers were so kind as to send me one of their beautiful books.

From Morristown I went across the country to Asheville, a very pretty town picturesquely situated in the mountains of Western North Carolina; then I continued on toward the coast, passing through Spartanburg, Columbia and Augusta. At Savannah I sailed for Fernandina, Florida, in the steamship *St. Johns*, and arrived in port on January 20, 1881.

I was warmly welcomed by kind friends whose acquaintance I had formed while sojourning there in the winter of 1879. The flowers were in bloom, the grass was delightfully refreshing to the eyes weary of gazing upon the snow-covered surface of the North, and the birds sang joyous and cheering melodies among the grand old moss-covered trees.

On the first day of February I walked out to the ocean-beach for the purpose of hunting shells, and the day was as warm and summer-like as is a June day in the Northern States.

On the beach I found the evidence of one of the most heart-rending phases of human suffering—a wreck at sea. The hull of the ship had been driven ashore by the wind and waves, and now lay upon the beach half buried in the sand. Pieces of masts, battered trunks, part of a life-preserver, a spool of thread and other remains of the ill-fated vessel, lay about upon the beach.

On returning homeward, I found the variations in the climate between Florida and the North quite interesting. I left Fernandina on the 3d of March,

a very warm day, while the earth was wrapped in a
mantle of luxuriant vegetation.   Upon arriving at
Savannah, there was a marked contrast in the air,
which was much cooler, and the grass and flowers
were not so forward.   At Charleston the weather
was still cooler, though the flowers were blooming.
Proceeding on to Wilmington, I found the weather
cold, and, during my stay there of one month, ice
formed several times.

I left Wilmington for Pennsylvania on the 16th
of April, and the air had by that time become warm
and genial, and Nature was arrayed in the beauty
of gorgeous spring-time; but one night's ride up
to Petersburg and Richmond, wrought a greater
change than I had yet experienced on the route,
both in the atmosphere and vegetation, the latter
having just began to push forth.   Upon reaching
Pennsylvania, the weather was harsh and cold, and
vegetation only began to show signs of life.

Soon after reaching my native state I proceeded
to Harrisburg and went into business, for I had resolved that when I stopped traveling and settled
down, I would locate in the capital city of dear old
Pennsylvania.

Harrisburg was laid out in 1785, by John Harris.
It is handsomely situated on the east bank of the
limpid Susquehanna, whose sparkling waters, and
the romantic hills and mountains through which it
flows, form one of the most pleasing and majestic

natural attractions to be found in the vicinity of any American city.

On the opposite side of the river, a mile from the din and commotion of the metropolis, can be seen quiet farm-houses, pretty, rural cottage-homes and enchanting groves and dells, wrapped in a sweet, serene calm that forms a most delightful contrast to the noisy, bustling city so near by.

Harrisburg is a great railroad center, and it is estimated that more than one hundred trains of cars arrive and depart, on the various roads, every day. The city is extensively engaged in manufacturing railroad-iron, various kinds of machinery, cars and other things of general and domestic use.

The population is thirty thousand. The place is surrounded by numerous little country towns, and some of the most thickly settled and wealthy farming country, in Pennsylvania.

The nature that loves to dwell in the sweet, poetical reverie that takes the mind far back to bygone times, can portray, in the imagination, the site of the city before the ever-advancing white man first planted his log hut upon its soil.

A ridge of lovely green bluffs on the background overlooked the river, into which flowed pretty rills, drained from springs on the mossy hillsides; the beautiful island in the river, now facing the city, was vocal with the melody of birds; the towering hills on the opposite shore, were adorned with the

garb of Nature; while the inviting groves echoed
with the laughter of Indian children at play, the
love-chants of dusky maidens, and the shrill whoop
of panting warriors; on the bosom of the noiseless
river glided the frail canoe, and in the deep forest
nestled the cozy, picturesque wigwam, from which
curled in graceful, waving ringlets the blue smoke
that served as a beacon to guide the weary hunter
home to wife and little ones.

This, you see, is a mind-picture, drawn by fancy,
but I ever have, and ever will have, such an affec-
tionate interest in the poor, oppressed red race,
and have so óften sojourned with them amid such
scenes, far from the haunts of white men, that, to
me, it appears to be a likely sketch of what existed
near the site of the present city of Harrisburg two
hundred years ago.

In traveling a person gets a knowledge of human
nature, a keen faculty of reading a face—the index
to the very heart and mind—almost as readily as he
would read a printed page. Indeed, a face might
be called the title-page to the inner work.

There is a saying to the effect that appearances
are sometimes deceiving, but this is a grave error
when applied to the human face. The dress and
general surroundings in life of a man, may deceive
many regarding his financial affairs, or intellectual
capacity, but his face does not indicate a certain
shade of character while in his heart and mind the

opposite exists. If we are deceived in a face, it is not because it is a false photograph of the inner being, but because we are not able to read it.

While I do not like the society of men near as well as I love to commune with books, the forests, the mountains, the birds, the flowers, I am an enthusiastic student of the many shades of mind and soul as expressed in the human face.

Selfishness, pride, unkindness and narrowmindedness go hand in hand, and form the worst traits in humanity. Unfortunately for those of us who are peace-loving people, for we must either "step upon, or be stepped upon," and as the heart of a kind, sensitive man or woman revolts at the idea of doings the former, we are at the mercy of any and every coarse, cruel, nature that desires to injure us with their vile, treacherous, slanderous tongue. A great and good writer once remarked that a gentle heart, like mellow fruit, hangs so low that any rude passer can pluck it.

About the only way to manage such creatures is to keep out of their company as much as possible. When we must come in contact with them, we can treat them kindly, but "hold them at a distance." A keen observer of human nature can "measure a man at a glance," and decide upon the course to be pursued in dealing with him.

Look into his face, his eyes especially, and take the dimensions of his soul. If you are at all ex-

pert, a moment will suffice to teach you what kind
of a person is before you. Whenever a man slily
scrutinizes your dress and person, with a cold, calculating eye, that never fails to indicate a vulgar,
dwarfed mind, and a selfish, unfeeling heart, utterly
destitute of the finer emotions of humanity, you
can conclude that it is best to form no deeper acquaintance with him.

They are the ones who are ever on the alert to
take advantage of you for their own gain, or always
ready to offer a sharp, bitter insult, or rehearse an
unkind, false report concerning another, or speak of
an absent party in suspicious, depreciating terms.
Never take such a creature into your heart or confidence, or you will make yourself liable to suffer
insult and mortification whenever they feel disposed
to offer it.

We should never believe a word such a person
says to the disadvantage of another, especially if
the slandered party is unknown to us, for he may
be a far better man than the prattler. My sympa-
thies invariably go toward the party thus injured,
and I have a much better opinion of them than I
have of the petty tattler.

After all, if we have nothing good to say about a
person, it would be perfect kindness and charity to
say nothing bad, and to bury their failings in the
deep oblivion of silence. People who talk much do
not, as a rule, have a profound regard for truth.

This fleeting life is far too short for hating, fault-finding, backbiting and the many vices that cling to our poor, weak nature. I often wonder at the love and patience the Almighty shows towards us, his thoughtless, disobedient creatures here. What are we that we should live so contrary to his will?

Surely, we are but a shell of clay, which, as soon as its immortal occupant leaves to test the realities of eternity, becomes a mere handful of repulsive matter that is hurriedly put under the ground, and there soon mingles with the dust, while the remaining caravan of humanity moves on its daily rounds, forgetting that the mouldering ashes in the gravo once occupied a place in its active ranks.

I now come to the end of my narrative, I shall roam no more. I have conquered the passion that ever prompts the restless rover to move. I have, I trust, settled down once for all, and in a quiet, peaceful life, diligence in business, and child-like trust in Him who ordereth all things well, I hope to find happiness, and contentment of mind that I never knew before.

Printed in the United States
80252LV00007B/121

9 781429 004497